A Journey of Riches

Making Changes

Table of Contents

Chapter 1: Tools For Change
By John Spender 1

Chapter 2: Letting My SELF Go - Dance like EVERYONE is watching
By Cassey Plouffe 23

Chapter 3: Forgiveness Is Power
By Marcia Miatke 39

Chapter 4: Awaken to Your Magnificence and the Magic All Around You
By John Abbott 53

Chapter 5: Passion is your Greatest Possession
By Goro Gupta 67

Chapter 6: Embracing Change
By Kiri Devi 83

Chapter 7: Change is the Only Way Forward
By Kelvin Kuan 109

Chapter 8: Never Give Up
By Teresa Elliott 123

Chapter 9: The Art of Becoming Resilient - My story, from my heart.
By Katrina Gulabovski 139

Chapter 10: Finding Your Purpose
By Dario Cucci 155

Chapter 11: It's Never Too Late
By Marina Marsden 165

Author Biographies 179

Chapter 1

Tools For Change

By John Spender

Making Changes

In this chapter I'm going share with you 12 principles that have helped me and many other people around the world to make successful changes. First of all lets treat change as an opportunity and with a positive outlook. Life is working for us and everything is happening for our greater good. You will find the principals easy to digest and to action.

Principal 1. Get a Mentor…..

If you always do what you've always done, you'll always get what you always gotten. That's a great quote by Tony Robbins and it's so true that we do the same routine and we expect different results. I love that quote and it's had a huge impact in so many people's lives, including my own and I often use it as a mantra. It's important that any time we desire to make a change, when we want to do something different, when we need to be different, that we have mentors that can actually guide us. Tony Robbins teachings are readily available through his books, online programs, through Youtube or his seminars. I've been to a number of his seminars, read his books and I watch him on YouTube. I feel he's just an awesome person to have influencing your life.

The late Dr. Wayne Dyer has been another person who has been a great mentor of mine. I've been to his workshops, keynote presentations and read his books and he really helped me change the way I viewed being kind to other people. A lot of the time when we want to make a change we need to step outside of our comfort zone. Working with someone who has already made the change that you aspire to make is a huge plus and it makes the transition so much easier. And let's face it, you know if we're not growing, we're dying; this is the whole evolution of the universe, we are meant to grow, we are meant to challenge ourselves, we are meant for adversity, so we can expand, grow and be a bigger version of ourselves.

One of Dr Dyer's favourite sayings was "Don't die with your music still inside you", and it's so true. I was in a cemetery in Los Angeles, just wondering through, and I pondered how many people had gone to the grave with their music unexpressed, with their gift inside, with their dream unfulfilled. I realised, you know what is worse than dying? it's dying with your potential not realised without even at least pursuing your dream, even if you don't succeed, at least you gave it a shot. Anytime I find myself caught between making a change or not, where I'm like 50-50, should I, should I not? I do the rocking chair test. The rocking chair test simply is; when I'm 90 years of age, sitting in my rocking chair on my front porch, would I regret not making that change, would I regret not pursuing that opportunity, would I regret not taking a risk or whatever it may be. And it really is an easy way to make a decision to make a change.

The hard part is facing the truth, the right choice is most often the most challenging path to choose, the correct answer can bring up a lot of emotions and fears. It normally means stepping up to be a bigger person and to play a bigger game. We can get caught up with wanting to know the outcome and if everything is going according to plan. And this is when we know that we are entertaining the HOW, the how of; is this going to work?, I wouldn't want xyz to happen, I'm not sure if I can do it. The how can also bring up fears like am I worthy, am I good enough, am I afraid of success? None of that is true, it's just the process of being stuck in the HOW.

A better alternative is to trust your truth and get excited about not knowing the outcome so much. I know what people say, that you need to plan and if you don't plan your planning to fail. I personally prefer to start with the desired outcome I'm looking for in any given situation. For all you die hard planners let me ask you a question. How many plans have you developed with great detail which have gone according to plan? The answer for me is never… not once! And I know what you die hard planners are saying, what about the contingency plan? Let go already, all that time you spent planning you could of had the task completed already. It's all about the end result baby and getting there any way you can.

When you know you need to make a change, you have a choice and it's like taking off a Band-Aid. You can either take it off slowly or you can take it off quickly, the choice is yours. Find your vision, refine it and let the universe take care of the how.

Principal 2. Set Clear Intentions…..

Intention deficit disorder, what does that mean exactly? Recently I caught up with Reverend Michael Beckwith for a film that I'm producing about discovering the gift in challenge. I interviewed him for about 40 minutes. If you haven't heard of him, he's worth looking up. He starred in the hit movie documentary "The Secret", he is the founder of the spiritual centre Agape in Los Angeles, California and he is just such an inspiring guy.

One of the many things that he said that resonated with me was his insight into people and humanity. He said that people suffer from an "intention deficit disorder". I find that to be true, a lot of people have no clear intention of what they would like to change in their life. Intention deficit disorder is a form of resistance to change, the passive kind. It's when you don't set an intention for your day, for your week, for your life. It's not having a clear intention of what is it that you are actually wanting to do in life. You know; what's your intention of having an intimate relationship, what's your intention with your career, what's your intention with your passion, what's your intention with things that you enjoy doing that make you come alive. I find that the more I set intentions for different aspects of my life the less dramatic and unsettling the changes I experience are. When you set intentions your resistance to change isn't as great and your focus and purpose for the bigger picture of your life can unfold naturally.

A perfect example would be: I set an intention one morning to start a new fitness regime with a desire to get super fit. In Bali, where I live, there is a local Freelectics group that meets twice a week. My intention was to make it through the Set; they have a Set of exercise's where they do a lot of jumping jacks, lunges and various intense exercises that get the heart rate pumping. My intention was just to finish, to just make it through and complete all the exercises. I'm usually the last to finish and most of the group finish early and don't complete the workout, it's literally go hard or go home and most of the group go home early. I just finished the two sets of exercises that I needed to do, 'cause that was my intention', it was a deliberate action that I set before I got out of bed, I set it the night before so I was clear when I woke up. Making the change from unfit to fit takes discipline and a deliberate action of setting an intention makes it so much easier. Initially it can be challenging and then you get into a routine and it becomes easier.

Have a single minded focus, have that intention for the day, and it's amazing how it actually plays out, how you allow the magic to unfold in the day.

The synchronicity that I've had with this film project has been incredible. I woke up one Sunday around the end of December 2015 and I just felt an overwhelming sense of fear and doubt. I started talking to my fear out loud saying that 'I need someone with film experience to give me some more in depth feedback on what I should do next'. I had just filmed a bunch of guests, but I felt like I was still finding my direction with the storyline. Off I went to play indoor cricket and I completely forgot about my conversation with my fear and doubt. We lost the cricket match in a close game. After the game I was introduced to this American guy who wanted to see what the game of Cricket was all about. We had a brief chat and that was it.

Most of the guys go to the local Aussie pub after every match and I usually go straight home as I rarely drink alcohol, on this occasion my intuition decided that I should go. When I arrived at the pub, I walked straight to the bar and ordered a fresh papaya juice and the America guy, Adam, was standing at the bar. He also wasn't drinking alcohol and was just standing by himself. We naturally started chatting and it turned out that he was a movie/documentary producer…Boom!! We chatted for a good hour and he was telling me about his current film project with all the different challenges they were facing and how they were overcoming them. He of course became an advisor for my documentary and I have come along in leaps and bounds with the project. I'm now talking to an award winning director about filming the drama scenes.

For me that's a perfect example of being willing to step into change and do something that I wouldn't normally do on many levels. When you incite change and even if it's scary at first, you are making changes by choice not changes that surprise the pants off you. Talk to your fears don't just listen to them and obey their commands, have a rational conversation with your fears and doubts and ask them to bring you you're ideal outcome. Now that you have set the intention, forget about it and expect magic to happen.

Principal 3. Stick To Your Commitments…..

Managing negative mind chatter can be tricky and frustrating to deal with at times, especially when your making changes or doing something for the first time. When I created the first "A Journey Of Riches" book, so many times I went through periods of self-doubt. What I found was the importance of saying daily affirmations, doing daily exercise, meditating daily and talking to friends who had written books and launched number one best sellers. My friends weren't going to do the work for me, but it certainly helped hearing their words of wisdom. Having daily routines that keep you healthy and happy are very important to controlling the negative mind chatter rather than it controlling you. Now this isn't new information and almost everyone knows it, but it's a whole anther story putting it into action.

This is a gap that can be too big to leap across at times and maintain the consistency required to achieve your desired outcome. When your desire is strong enough, the drive and motivation flows naturally and keeping your mind, body and spirit sharp becomes easier. The enjoyment of your routines is another key factor in sticking with it. When it comes to affirmations I keep them very simple and some of my favourites are;

What ever the mind can conceive and believe it can achieve.
~ Napoleon Hill

I love the highest and best in all people, I now draw the highest and best people to me.
~ Unknown

I love and appreciate myself.
~ Louise Hay

Everything is always working out for me.
~ Abraham/Esther Hicks

In times of self-doubt I would say these affirmations in blocks of 50 times each throughout the day. What happens as a result, your belief begins to soar and your confidence grows and the action steps become easier to take.

Showing up is one of the most important steps because there is no chance of you getting a result, any kind of result, if you don't at least show up. You know that sometimes we don't feel like showing up and taking action. You have to do the task at hand first and then the feeling of satisfaction comes afterward. I don't always feel like doing certain aspects of putting together a book but when I take action despite my mood the feeling of enjoyment finds me quickly and even more so when I start to make progress.

I can't encourage and enthuse enough the importance of showing up, just doing small little action steps. Once you understand your mission, you have an intention, or something that you must finish, having discipline becomes second nature. A well known challenge though is as we come to the end of a project, get close to completion of whatever it may be, we just fade a little bit, and it is at this time too many people quit, when the end is near. The principal I learned from Robert Kayasaki is just keep turning up and under achieving, that's right under achieving. I know this sounds counter intuitive so let me explain with an example. You want to establish a new habit, just say you want to get fit and go to the gym for instance. When you're at the gym, you might do one exercise, you might do the bike for 15 minutes, and then go home. This is really easy and actually leaves you wanting more, it leaves you thinking, why can't I do more? I can do more. When I get writers block I will just write 300 words and that's it, it doesn't even have to make sense and this small action creates momentum. Soon enough my writing begins to flow. It's creating a game where winning is easy and before you know it you're in the zone.

I also know that sometimes we need to take extended breaks, we need to take a breather from our commitments before we start new ones, we need to chill, relax and recharge the batteries. Just recently I was able to combine my commitments and include time to recharge. I went to the U.S. to work on the current film I'm producing where we were interviewing and filming Jack Canfield, Casey Plouffe and Jessica Cox, an amazing women who was born without arms. I went for a month and I was able to have time off between shoots and do some sightseeing and relax. This enabled me to be fresh and alert on all the interviews I did for the film. Recharging the batteries is a gift that we all deserve to give ourselves and at times it becomes a necessary change to make. It certainly allows me to come back to whatever I'm doing bigger, better and realigned to my purpose with increased focus.

Principal 4. You don't need fixing…..

You don't need fixing, you are not broken, you are perfect just the way you are! I know, I hear it; but this, but that, but I got angry last week. Everything is playing out as a divine higher purpose, everything is a gift if you are open enough to see it. If we open our hearts enough to see it, there's a gift in every action. No more beating yourself up, no more berating yourself, no more but ifs, no more perfection. Isn't it true that we find perfection when we embrace what "is", we accept what "is", and we accept the perfection in the imperfection, and nature does this perfectly.

I was recently in Singapore where I spent an hour or so in nature. It was simply beautiful, just the connection to the wild life and the plants, birds came straight up to me and fish swam to me as well. I wasn't thinking…. if only I did this, if I only had that or this was missing from my life, I wasn't focusing on outside circumstances. I was just being present in the moment and allowed nature to come to me. It was so peaceful and so serene. I think that knowing we are the thinker of our thoughts along with the feeler of our emotions, this empowers us to know that we are alright as we are.

Self-sabotaging behaviours and that little voice sometimes just seems incessant and just won't give up! We need to be our own best friend. Back in early 2000 in one of her audios Louise Hay said, be still with yourself and be your own best friend. Be kind to yourself, speak words of encouragement and praise yourself. When you start to do this it is much easier for you to praise and be encouraging to other people. Things start to shift and change, not only do you start to like your soul but you begin to start to like others more as well. Generally if a person has no friends it's because they don't like themselves, they don't like anyone. See your greatness, see your beauty, recognize your awesomeness, start seeing it in other people and you'll awaken it within yourself.

Principal 5. Believe In Yourself…..

What I've found that really made a difference when I was transitioning from my landscaping business into coaching, speaking, writing, and now making my first movie, was to actually help other people that didn't believe in themselves. That's right, there's so many people out in the world that have low self-esteem with their belief and with self-worth much lower than yours. Helping them helps you as you are going through your transition or major change, especially if it is something to do with your career, which was my case.

I basically volunteered my time at Mission Australia, in Sydney, helping people that were borderline homeless in crisis situations and were just hard out on their luck. A lot of them were on drugs, or medicated on drugs and all different types of concoctions of things to actually help them maintain a level of stability. When I went in there I was learning NLP at the time, neuro-linguistic-programming, and I had just finished my practitioner's training certificate. I shared to the group what I knew, at that stage I had never done any public speaking before in my life and

I thought I was going to die; really, it was super scary, but you know what? I got in front of those people and I was super surprised at the difference that I was making. My self-belief went through the roof, it was sky high after that and it wasn't too long after this experience I received my first paying coaching client.

What I recommend to people first of all is to help those that have less belief than you do. If they have low self-esteem, lower confidence or are more fearful, help them and your confidence, your self-belief, your self-esteem will soar as a result.

Another thing I recommend is to do something that you love to do every day. It can be very hard to find the time to do something that you enjoy, that you are passionate about and that you just can't wait to jump out of bed to do. When you do find the time you will see it's very hard to do those sort of activities and to feel self-doubt, to feel fear and to self-sabotage yourself simultaneously because you are doing something that you enjoy, something that you love, something that makes your spirit soar. I strongly recommend to my coaching clients when they are wanting to raise their self-belief is to seek out people or a situation to support or volunteer their time to a not for profit organization in any way they can. Plus do one thing daily that brings happiness and joy to your life.

Another thing that I like to do here in Bali is volunteer my time at the orphanage, Hope Children's Home. That's just a fantastic experience, there's a lot of kids there that are very sad. On the outside they can be very happy, but when you talk to them and dig a little bit deeper, there's a lot of disappointment there left unexpressed. Being around kids and people that are less fortunate than yourself can make a huge difference to their life and also your own. This can really set you on your path to increase belief in yourself and help you to transition through your own change and growth.

Principal 6. Cure Yourself Of Excusitis…..

What is excusitis and how can you overcome it? Excuse-itis, how often have you gone to do something and you haven't followed through, you found an excuse instead. For example, you made a decision that you were going to go jogging 4 days a week, and you are good for the first week, then the 2nd week you miss two days and then you find it's almost impossible to go jogging early in the mornings again. The excuses that come up are endless; you forgot to set the alarm, you just didn't feel like it, you ate way to much at dinner the night before, whatever it may be. It's one of the largest forms of resistance there is to making changes in one's life.

This word has been taken from the famous book, "The Magic of Thinking Big" by David Schwartz – Chapter Two – Cure Yourself of Excusitis, the Failure Disease. He uses the word "EXCUSITIS" (from the root word "excuse"), which he defined as "The disease of the failures." He said that, "Every failure has this disease in its advanced form." And yes it's contagious, if your close friends are always making excuses, you will eventually do the same.

One of the things that I work on with some of my clients is how to overcome excusitis and become aligned to their values, dreams and desires. You need to take away all the excuses, you need to make it as easy as possible to get rid of the excuses and to form a new habit, goal or whatever it may be.

First of all you need to have an accountability partner, someone who's going to keep you accountable. This can be as simple as checking in each week, having a weekly review to see what's happening and if you're being true to your commitment. The chances of you letting yourself down by not doing the new habit are pretty high actually, but the chances of you letting someone else down as well as yourself is lower, your chances of success increase. Most people don't want to let a good friend down.

The **second** thing is develop a bigger reason for forming the new habit, what is the purpose for forming the new habit? Going jogging a few times a week could be the new habit. This could be because you're over the fact that when you are playing with the kids in the park you're absolutely puffed after ten minutes, your totally exhausted and you can't continue and you feel embarrassed. This means you're missing connection time with your children, that's a pretty strong purpose, a strong motivator and reason to actually go running in the mornings and to get fit. The secret is you need to attach it to something that's important and significant to you that's worthwhile doing.

Thirdly, you want to make a public declaration, declare to as many people as possible that you are actually going to set a new habit, a new routine or whatever it may be. You need to declare what this is and what you are going to do because then you won't want to look silly in front of a whole bunch of people, that's why you need to declare your intention. I've done this on Facebook and also when I was taking part in a speaker and trainers program back in late 2010 in Sydney.

The program went over 5 days and the second last night was called outrageous night. This is where the 180 participants got dressed up in outrageous costume and then had to sing a 2 minute song of our choice on stage. We were divided into two groups of around 90 people each and the instruction was to express yourself in any way that would be a challenge for you. How it worked was the MC would call someone to the stage and then there would be another three people lined up next to the stage ready to sing their song.

I wanted to be the best speaker that I could develop into and I wanted to give myself the ultimate challenge. When they called my name out to line up everyone started to cheer but this quickly faded as everyone was in fancy dress except me. People were disappointed at my lack of effort. As I stood in line I began to take off my shoes, socks and my T-shirt. As I moved second in line I took off my jeans and a few people started to take notice and I saw them pointing at me and talking to each other. Even before that I was having heart palpitations and it felt like I was going to die. I started counting four seconds on my in breath, holding for four seconds, breathing out for four seconds and holding my breath for another four seconds. This breathing technique was my saviour. It was now my turn to stand first in line ready to go on stage. Remember I was standing there in my underwear. As the MC called my name to go on stage I whipped off my underwear and walked onto the stage in my birthday suit!!

The loud gasp from the 90 odd people in the audience rang through my ears as I stood on stage completely naked.

Before each person could sing their song and act outrageously you had to stand on stage with your arms wide open completely exposed to receive an energy woosh. This is when the audience clap their hands together three times and after the third clap, projected their energy and arms out towards you while making a woosh sound.

My adrenaline began to kick in and I don't remember feeling the energy woosh, but I remember feeling very supported and the looks of disbelief, encouragement and excitement will stay with me forever. I also remember not wanting to look down as the air conditioning made the room very cold, like very cold. Time was in slow motion until I started singing 'Relax don't do it' by Frankie Goes to Hollywood and I was jumping all over the stage singing the chorus over and over again. That didn't matter as the crowd were going crazy banging on the stage, wolf whistling and cheering with excitement.

Before I knew it the music stopped but the cheering and excitement kept on ringing through my ears, with my heart pumping fast and filled with excitement, shame and euphoria all rolled into one. Again I had to stand with my arms wide open and receive an energy woosh..... I had never been so exposed in my whole life and also so accepted in my entire life, it was so overwhelming. In the break I had several woman that I never met before wanting to hug and kiss me.

It was such a surreal experience and I don't think I would have done it if I didn't tell my friends in my group what I was going to do. I told at least 5 of them and I tried to encourage them to do it too, but they were like no way!! There was no chance I could back out, the pain of them teasing me or seeing me as a person who was all talk and no action was greater than me challenging myself and going on stage naked. Now when I'm on stage at different venues around the world I speak with my clothes on!

The **fourth** thing is you want to have a reward, a reward for following through, it could be that you get to go out on a date-night with your wife to your favourite restaurant, whatever it may be the reward needs to be good. I treated myself to all I could eat sushi after my nude singing performance.

The **fifth step** is you need to have a consequence, that's right! a consequence, for not following through. It could be your neighbor gets to put a cream pie in our face, or it could be that you'll donate to a particular political party, a political party that you just hate and it would be an absolute nightmare for you to have to shell out some coin from your wallet to this political party that you can't stand. The thought of the consequence should just disgust you so that it is a strong incentive to keep your word.

To recap in how to overcome excusitis and make any change in your life;

1. *Accountability partner*,
2. *Declare* to many people and even post your intention on social media,
3. Have a *strong reason/purpose* to drive you forward,
4. *Reward*, the greater the risk the greater the reward,
5. Have a *deterrent/consequence*, a strong motivator.

So there you have it, my fundamentals for overcoming excuse-itis and to make lasting change.

Principal 7. Priority Management.....

I'm too busy, I hear that all the time. Different projects that I'm working on and there are deadlines, people tell me "I've just been so busy". What it really comes down to, is priority management, prioritising your schedule, prioritising the things that you need to get done because, let's face it, everyone's busy, even my mum who's retired is busy. If you become sick you would go to the doctor, you wouldn't say I'm too busy to go to the doctor…no, you make it a priority and you go to the doctors. It's not time management that's needed when making changes it's priority management. It's impossible to manage time, you can manage what you do within your time though. When you've got your priorities right change can seem effortless and you hardly notice it.

When dealing with change or challenging circumstances priority management is your best friend. What I do is list the top five things that I want to get one for the day, and then get them out of the way, take them off the list. This creates momentum and takes care of the busyness feelings.

Busyness really comes down to fear, it's an excuse and what you are really saying is the task wasn't a high enough priority or maybe you felt too afraid to tackle it, you didn't feel up to that task. I challenge you, for tomorrow or for this week, I challenge you to prioritise your day, list the tasks that are the highest priority and get them out of the way first.

The problem is when we are in a state of fear it's easy to get busy, it's easy to check social media, it's easy to get distracted, and distraction stops us from facing the task at hand. Quite often there's a fear associated with doing the task and fears can be embedded deep into the subconscious mind, that's why we avoid doing it. Filling your day with meaningless activities is a symptom of fearing change. Change isn't the problem it's the fear of change, of the unknown and wanting to stay safe. Becoming organised and prioritising our day can help to bring our fears to the surface so we can face the fear, process it and move on.

Principal 8. Tap Into Your Inner Happy…..

Happiness and laughter are two of the best tools to use when making and going through stressful changes. One of the easiest forms of happiness is instant gratification and it's an external happiness, a happiness that we find outside of ourselves. It can also be a distraction from making the necessary changes needed to get the result you deserve. One of the easiest ways to do this is to purchase a new handbag, to buy a new aftershave and to basically buy things that you don't need.

It can act as a distraction and that instant feeling of happiness and satisfaction doesn't last as long as finding a deeper source of happiness. You purchase something, you feel good, you become tired of that item or whatever it is, and then you need something else to purchase, you need to stick something else on the credit card and potentially get into more debt.

The best form of happiness is happiness that comes from within. It's internal happiness and you probably know this, you've heard it before, but are you actually tapping into it? Going within and finding happiness from the inside out, rather than the outside in. Being happy with who you are as a person, your good and bad traits, making peace with yourself. Change becomes easier to manage when you have a deep well of happiness emanating from inside you. I know that we're spiritual beings having a human experience and that we have all that we need within ourselves, we don't need external factors to actually make us happy, everything we need is within us.

We can tap into our own source of happiness, our own richness, our own goodness, our own abundance. It's just like breathing, you don't have to think about it and you have a right to feel happy. A deep sense of happiness comes from having a purpose, having a mission greater than one self and you feel alive ready to take on any challenge.

Principal 9. Do Something You Love To Do Everyday…..

This may seem counter intuitive when you're going through dramatic changes in your life, but it's the best medicine. It's so easy to get caught up in our stories and routines, and sometimes that routine just gives you a certain level of sameness, that we are doing the same old thing. I know before I came over to Bali to live, my life back in Australia was awesome. I had a great life, lived in a great suburb and had awesome friends. It was just that sometimes, for me, life seemed like the same old things, driving the same car, living in the same place, going to work at the same time, socialising with the same friends, and it created a little bit of mundaneness.

It becomes important to make a change or we can get caught up in the same old routine and feel unhappy and not even know why we feel unhappy or stale. One of the things that I do, even in Bali, is to get out and travel a lot and explore different parts of the island. I like to do something that I love every day, so I meditate or exercise in the morning and catch the sunrise, then catch the sunset in the afternoon and catch up with friends and have fun.

I'm mindful of changing up my routines of doing something that I love every day and I'm actually pretty good at it now. There was definitely a time, when I was living in Sydney and I was travelling, I would come back home and I was like "hmmm"….. it was almost like an addiction that I wanted to just be somewhere new and fresh.

I've discovered a way of handling the same old thing and discovering a newness. One of the things that I would do when driving to the same landscaping job, or whatever it was, I would go a different way, take a different route on my journey and it created a sense of difference. I would look for things that maybe I hadn't noticed before, things that I appreciate and that I enjoy. I encourage you this week, rather than driving the same way to work or taking the same form of transportation to mix it up a little bit. Maybe you could get a lift to work with a buddy. If you have to drive try taking a different route to your job. You'll be surprised by the freshness you'll feel just by changing your routines up a little.

It's very easy to be caught in the mundaneness of a 9 to 5, or a 7 to 4, or whatever it maybe. There is a way that you can actually mixed it up, so there's a bit of newness, a bit of freshness and with the newness and freshness that you bring into your routine you will start feeling a lot more appreciation for different things that you already have in your life. Who doesn't like a little bit of freshness and newness and as the saying goes "change is as good as a holiday", so change up your routine this week and enjoy the experience.

Principal 10. Take a Chance on Yourself…..

We miss all the shots that we don't take, at some point in our lives we need to actually back ourselves and take a chance on life. Now Michael Jordan is famous for saying that "every shot that you don't take, you miss" and it's an undeniable truth from a great man, one of the greatest players to play the game of basketball. What is it that stops us from taking opportunities? Why are we so comfortable in our comfort zones? I believe that there is a 2 year old child in each and every one of us, and it loves comfort, it loves instant gratification, it loves certainty and it loves knowing what's gonna happen next. The thing is opportunities are mostly on the other side of that comfort zone. Opportunities to our child mind can often mean change and change means danger and the mind can create a storm, expecting a rough time. That's the mind of a two year old child, it wants to keep us safe, it wants to create certainty, it wants comfort, it wants instant gratification, but at some point we need to take a chance on ourselves, as everything happens on the other side of our comfort zone.

At the end of 2010 when my coaching practice was taking off, I set another goal of becoming an international trainer with T Harv Ecker and Success Resources Global run a program every year in Thailand called Making The Stage. The cost to attend this course is $10k usd, a fair investment. My desire was strong but not my preparation and I fell short of being chosen. Although I was disappointed another opportunity presented itself to me in April 2011 with Chris Howard in Los Vegas and after 10 days of training and a fair investment I fell short again. I was so much closer this time and the disappointment was harder to deal with and it was another 20 months before I received an opportunity to achieve my goal.

In the long interval I had joined toastmasters and I went in all their speaking contests. I also started my own speaking group practicing in my lounge room. At the end of 2011 I held my first intro event for my coaching programs with mix results. At the end of 2012 I received a message from one of Chris Howard's staff about joining his new start up in Bali. The initial agreement was for 3 months with no pay, only my accommodation and food would be covered. I would be given an opportunity to lead various trainings in Singapore and Bali.

It was a big decision to make and at the same time it wasn't. I had been praying for an opportunity like this for a while at that point. It was a big decision at the time, but I decided to make the change and take the leap of faith. Looking back, it was the best decision and although there were many challenges, I ran a few trainings' in Singapore and achieved my goal.

I remember the first training that I ran in Singapore we were due to start at 6am in the morning but the day before I was in bed with a fever and I had lost my voice. I mean I couldn't say a word and after sleeping all afternoon and night, I was up and ready in the morning feeling pumped.

I absolutely nailed the training and I received glowing feedback from the students. Although it was a great experience and I ran a few more trainings I'm not really an indoors person. It was awesome to achieve the goal of becoming an international trainer and I learnt that persistence pays off in the long run. I also made many new friends and after not accepting Chris's offer of a six month contract I decided to stay in Bali and go back to my coaching practice running it online.

It can be painful to make changes, it can be painful to take a chance on ourselves, to believe in ourselves and to step on that edge, that edge where we could fly or fall flat on our face. Every time I have taken a chance on myself, even if I didn't get the desired result I've been all the better for it. Having a clear vision enabled me to see the obstacles as necessary steps to shape me into the person who was capable of living the desired goal.

Principal 11. Find an Excuse to Have Fun…..

I think that so often it is very easy to take our lives too seriously, especially when we are focused on our goals, intentions and visions for our future. With this focus we can forget to make time to have fun and to laugh, for no good reason, just because you can, just because it feels good to have a good laugh, to let the inner playful soul come out and run amuck. It's too easy to worry and it doesn't change anything at all, it keeps things the same and maybe that's the payoff for people, they get to stay the same. When we stay relaxed and believe in ourselves and laugh, it's infectious and it releases all different types of chemicals and endorphins in the body, like serotonin and it just makes you feel good. It's healthy and it's been known to heal people from diseases. Take the example shown in the movie - documentary "The Secret", where a woman with cancer and her husband watched funny movie's all day long, she laughed herself to health. Also the late Norman Vincent Peel, he had tuberculosis as a child and he laughed himself to health, so laughter really is a powerful natural medicine, and it's fun!

Let that inner child come out and play! I turned 40 this year, but I'm really a 4 year old child. I give myself permission to go out and have fun. Sometimes I also take things way too seriously and I've gotta catch myself and just remind myself that" Hey, it's time to have a bit of fun, it's time to let the inner child come out and play." On all our film and interview sets we have fun by keeping things as light as possible. At the end of each shoot we do group photo's with all the crew and the guest making funny faces. The one with Jack Canfield was a classic, he's a man who has achieved so much and he is always looking for new ways to have fun. He shared with us that he will watch 10 minutes of comedy a day! He then gave everyone a signed copy of his book " The Success Principals". I'm not sure if that wouldn't of happened if we didn't dare to have fun with him.

If you find yourself at different times getting a little bit too serious, don't forget to laugh and to laugh out loud. Make silly jokes just to be playful, it really makes a big difference to your stress levels and it makes a big difference to your relationships and your friendships. Have fun, for no good reason, just because you can.

Change doesn't have to be a swear word, in fact change can be your best friend!

Principal 12. Be Grateful For Your Current Situation…..

It doesn't matter where we find ourselves in life, we can find something to improve. Life is forever expanding, changing, dying and birthing, every living organism is doing the same. The single most important state of mind that you can practice is love and gratitude for everything in your life, starting from the moment that you wake up.

The very situation that we deem challenging now, later in time turns out to be a blessing. Being in a state of gratitude is like being in heaven and it fosters peace, harmony and big picture thinking. It allows us to see all prospectives, viewpoints and truths regarding our circumstances, situations and brings us into present moment awareness the here and the now. Right in this moment how many challenges, issues or changes do you have to make? Not many right your reading this book, occasionally your mind might drift away from reading, but you bring yourself back to the here and now. That's an important gift of gratitude, a feeling of presence, of aliveness, of connection and peace.

If you haven't heard of Dr John DeMartini he is worth looking up, his teaching's are deep, meaningful and practical. One of his rituals he does every morning before he gets out of bed, is to recite all the things that he is grateful for in his life. He doesn't get out of bed until a tear of gratitude appears for all he has in his life. Can you imagine doing that every morning? And for sure this is one of the reasons why he is an amazing man and impacts so many people in a positive way. Personally I like to take short moments throughout out the day to acknowledge how amazing life is and to breathe deeply into my lungs and to give thanks. Even 30 seconds of doing this can bring us into a state of gratitude.

Maybe keeping a gratitude journal is your thing and every evening before you sleep you recite what you are grateful for in life. What ever it is when you make getting into a state of gratitude part of your daily routine, you will notice that you'll become happier, healthier and experience greater levels of peace. I hope you continue to expand yourself, to step into challenges with a positive mind-set and put the above principals into practice on this wonderful journey we call life.

Chapter 2

Letting My SELF Go
Dance like EVERYONE is watching.

By Cassey Plouffe

"Let's go spend an hour in the champagne room."

As the saying goes, "If I had a dollar for every time I uttered that line, I'd be rich!" Not so long ago, I was adorned by a nightly uniform that consisted of a nylon g-string, clear acrylic stilettos and enough caked-on make-up to rival a drag queen. When I took the stage under that glittery disco ball and flashing strobe lights, I discovered that I could create a fantasy world of escapement that was as enticing for me as it was for the multitudes of men who threw dollar bills at my feet like rose petals, but the strip club smelled nothing like roses. Even now, the aroma of stale cigarettes and cheap cologne instantly remind me of the house of lies that helped form my ego as a rebellious (yet ambitious!) young woman.

I was the most "successful" teenager I knew. Whilst my friends' parents were teaching them the responsibility of managing money and how money doesn't grow on trees, all I needed was my fake ID and the following of devoted "regulars" and the club became my ATM. Like most teenagers, I was living under the usual influences: alcohol, recreational drugs, and probably the most dangerous of all – the need to be a part of the "in crowd".

Growing up as a pale, freckled-faced red-head, pretty wasn't a part of the reflection in my mirror, but in the club, that all changed. When I was on the stage, my freckles faded away. Adoration, acceptance, stacks of money, and hanging with the "wrong crowd" was more than enough for me to feel a part of the "in crowd". I remember that transition from kidhood into a blossoming young woman…I thought that I had really found myself; who I truly was. But let me be clear, I didn't set out with my life goal to be a stripper; although there IS something to be said for the education that I received as a pseudo-entrepreneur! I was resourceful, driven, and had managed to find a way to make more money than all of my friends combined. But after years of being in that environment, I began to feel dead inside. The same thing that had once made me feel so self-assured and alive was now killing me. But if not a carefree, crowd-pleasing dancer, then who would I be? At the time, I didn't have the answer to that question…but what I did have was the courage and ambition to make a change. Come to think of it, that's something that I've always had.

I've discovered that some of the greatest gifts ever received have come from mustering the courage to jump off the cliff versus just peering over the edge of it. Sometimes that courage comes from a voice that's deep within us, yet other times it comes from getting a helpful push from the ones who love us. I will be forever grateful for my loving parents who made it possible for me to hear the voice that was deep inside of me, which was urging me not to disappoint them. Getting that nudge to leave the land of adult entertainment and go to school to establish a "respectable" career as a nurse took a leap of faith that has resulted in great success. But I would be remiss not to acknowledge that my success is not entirely of my own volition, rather it is due much in part to the faith that my parents have always had in me.

If I've learned anything in my life, it's that there's one thing that seems to always remain the same: Change! And paradoxically, change is also the one thing that we as knucklehead human beings most often tend to resist. But why is that? I believe the answer is simple, it's because venturing outside of our comfort zone and into our true destiny is scary as hell! Those feelings of the unknown and the unfamiliar creep into our sympathetic nervous system and urge us to follow the proverbial instructions, "If it ain't broke, don't fix it!" "Stay put, where it's nice and safe."

But the truth of the matter is, despite all of our fears, our souls always know better. I have continuously found value in being accepted, independent, and in birthing the ambition to achieve what I perceive as success through continuously embracing change. And it is through this loving embrace that I have repeatedly received my greatest gifts!

Now let's get real…no matter how strong our will is, some changes just take a little more time than others to come to fruition. For instance, my transition from stripper extraordinaire to nurse was one of those slow, steady changes. Knowing all of the things that I do now, I've stopped myself from wanting to press that invisible fast forward button in order to get to the good stuff in my life just a little bit quicker. If I had only known back then what I do now… But you know what? There have been so many invaluable lessons and blessings that have been brought to me from all those years of ups and downs. Without a doubt, there's something to be said for life experience, and needing to walk the path that lies before us in the very way that it presents itself. I no longer wish for life to move faster because I've learned that making the most of life in the here and now is what makes the journey the sweetest. Just as a caterpillar takes time to blossom into a butterfly, making the change from stripper to author, motivational speaker, and top income earner in network marketing was a transition that required a careful metamorphosis of my Self. But what came out of that cocoon was the real truth.

As a teenager moving into adulthood, I discovered that ambition was the primary driver of change in my life. I figured out how to make all the right moves to get ahead. But ambition brought mostly external rewards, and as I continued to mature, I found myself noticing that the more important changes would be the ones that would affect me on the inside.

"When you change the way you look at things, the things you look at change." - Dr. Wayne W. Dyer

I imagine that if having the courage to bust out of our comfort zone is the first step to embracing change, then being open to developing a new perspective isn't too far behind. Seeing things in a brand new light and having those "Aha! moments" is indeed one of the greatest gifts of all. It never ceases to amaze me how two people can share the same experience whereby one person perceives it as a blessing and a gift, while the other sees it only as a curse. Make no mistake this is a choice that we are in complete control of!

This notion of developing a new perspective sprung to life for me during my career as a registered nurse. I had scheduled some time off to vacation in Mexico with my boyfriend (now husband!) and his family. As we toured through the remote, poverty-stricken villages, my overblown ego was quieted and sheepishly put into check. Surrounded by a world of struggle and lack, I suddenly felt like an ungrateful, spoiled brat. Flashbacks of my childhood surfaced, reminding me of the embarrassment I felt as my parents drove me to private school every day in their shabby, broken down cars. I thought about how, instead of being accepted amongst the "in crowd" circles, I was rejected and ridiculed for wearing sneakers with no swoosh on the side and jeans with no name stitched on the back pocket.

But there I was, touring a third-world country and seeing families living in deteriorating huts with no electricity, no running water, and no glimmer of hope for a better tomorrow. WOW! How blind and selfish could I have been to have taken my good fortune for granted when in actuality, I had everything that I really needed?!

At that very moment, my mind's eye opened wide, allowing a state of sincere gratitude to sink deeply into my heart. My resentments of the have-nots of my past and holding myself in higher esteem for "having made it" quickly dissolved and were replaced with thoughts of gratitude and humility. The change in perspective that resulted from my experiences in Mexico birthed a massive shift in my overall thinking and altered the course of my life. Knowing true gratitude is one the of greatest gifts I have ever received from allowing changes to occur in my perspective. Sometimes it's not the people who change, it's the mask that falls off.

Getting back to nursing, this was a time when I was in the process of revamping my Self into a respectable, responsible woman. I had managed to make the jump from the stage to the hospital, which is precisely where I realized that I was taking for granted what I now consider to be one of the greatest forms of wealth - my health. Working the night shift and caring for sick adults by lifting, bending and twisting them around in their hospital beds eventually took its toll on me with a thrown-out back. At the ripe ol' age of 26, I found myself injured and on medical leave, wondering what I would do next. After hearing my story, my doctor advised that I make the switch to pediatrics immediately, which led me to a position in pediatric oncology.

Working with children battling cancer was the last thing I would have chosen as my career, but as with most challenges, there are great lessons to be learned. This was a place that enveloped me with reminders of the value and necessity of living in a constant state of gratitude. I used to perceive my back injury as a stumbling block to the career that I had worked so long and hard for; but now it serves as one of the most vivid reminders that brings me right back to the wise Wayne Dyer: "When you change the way you look at things, the things you look at change."

Through caring for children dying of cancer, one can't help but to be clobbered over the head with thoughts of "what really matters" in life. Up until this point, I had not put nearly the level of value on my own health that I should have, and my own health was suffering as a result of it. I was more than a few pounds overweight and looking for my own personal solution to improved health. Knowing this, my friend Jennifer told me that I should take a look at some products that she had been using as a way to lose weight, feel great, and earn some extra money. I reluctantly took her advice, and after 5 days of experiencing this superfood nutrition and eliminating all of the crap that had built up in my body over the years, I WAS HOOKED! This was the catalyst for the next major change in my life. l will never forget reading the book "Detoxify or Die" by Dr. Sherry Rogers, which left me feeling more like a murderer than a nurse. Pumping bags of chemo into these sweet children's bodies didn't help ease my conscience any. Feeling hypocritical and convicted on a daily basis, I set out on a personal mission to get educated about the nutrition and healthy lifestyle that had been introduced to me.

I began learning more about holistic approaches to healthcare rather than relying completely on medicine. The hopeless gazes coming from the eyes of those children that I thought I was helping seemed to be crying out, "please…no more. I just want to go home." It was in those unforgettable moments when it became clear to me that it was the chemo that was really killing them - not the cancer. I plunged even further into nutritionally-based reading and studying in hopes of discovering a magic recipe to help improve the health of these precious patients, as well as for myself and others.

The more I read, the more I knew that I could not continue with the status quo. I was on fire about my new passion for nutrition! The world needed saving from its health crisis, and I would be the one to save it! From what I had experienced, the benefits of the product ingredients that I had been consuming were undeniable and I found myself wanting nothing more than to spread the word to as many people as I could.

Soon, after a little more persistent nudging from my friend, I began to investigate the business opportunity that was associated with these products. Why not get paid by turning others on to the nutrition that was so positively changing my life? Here's where the "gotcha" comes in…this business opportunity turned out to be Network Marketing! My first thought was "No way in hell would I be caught dead by getting involved with a 'pyramid scheme' business", which is what I had been hearing from everyone as well.

Besides, how much money could one really make from selling some health products anyway? Would I be dialing for dollars? Stalking my family and friends to be my first customers? What about going back to school for my masters degree? What about all of the time, energy and money that I had already invested in my nursing career? After all, if I wasn't a respectable, responsible nurse, then who would I be?

Despite all of my questions and doubts, I couldn't seem to quiet that little voice deep down inside of me that was softly whispering, "But Casey…WHAT IF???" What if this really was that vehicle that could lead me to financial freedom like I had been hearing about? What if all of those other people's success stories were legitimate and my stubborn skepticism was the only thing standing in the way of me creating my own story of happiness and the ability to live life on my terms versus at the mercy of others?

After researching the products even more, continuing to use them, and seeing firsthand how great they made my body feel, the decision to change careers quickly became a no-brainer, and I knew from that all too familiar feeling in my gut that it was time to take that jump once again. I had found a nutritional system that was a true game changer, and surely there were thousands of others out there who were looking for the same thing. Once I opened myself up to sharing this system with other hopefuls who were looking for a solution to regain their health, I not only found the key to my financial vault, but even more importantly, I discovered the key to my personal vault - the one that is now allowing me to live a life full of divine purpose, unlimited freedom, and incomparable personal fulfillment! You may be wondering how I was able to make such a courageous leap of faith. Well, it all starts with a little thing called mindset.

When one door closes, another door opens.

I am so thankful that I decided to become completely open to the idea of being a network marketer and was able to embrace everything the industry had to offer. If you know anything at all about Network Marketing as a profession, you're likely aware of the cultural differences from that of Corporate America and even the medical industry. It's like apples and oranges! Utilizing intra-team competition and political red tape to get ahead had now become a thing of the past. As a network marketer, I was introduced to such concepts as personal development, vision boarding, and co-creating my life by some of the most impactful mentors of my life thus far. I credit both Lenny Evans and Dave MacArthur as two leaders who not only taught me, but also showed me by example, how to cast a vision through being of massive service to others in order to realize true success. I had no idea how much being exposed to personal development at such a deep level would utterly rock my world!

That said, these ideas were brand new to me, and radically different than anything that I had ever been taught as a child in Catholic school. Unlike this new create-your-own-life mentality, I was taught that the life that we live is dealt to us like a hand of cards and is somewhat predetermined; meaning, if my parents weren't millionaires, then there's a pretty good chance that I wouldn't be one either. I shared the common belief that I was born in sin, must repent regularly for acting in sin, and that God is an external force that I must be fearful of. With the help of my new-found spiritual leaders, I began to open my mindset to ideas such as "God is within us", or that "we are able to have anything that we desire according to the thoughts that we think". These mentors taught me that our thoughts and feelings are created first from our state of BEing. "What a man thinks, so shall he be." And it is our thoughts that produce the circumstances that are happening all around us; therefore, if there's something wrong with my life, then I can only surmise that I am applying wrong thinking!

But the proverbial icing on the cake was what they taught me about the value of belief and expectation. In order to manifest real change in our lives, it is imperative to have 100% belief that our new thoughts are not only possible, but they are a FACT; and allowing even 1% doubt is equal to having 0% faith. And faith (which is something I had lost) is what produces a thing called certainty. On fire about my new super powers, I began working nonstop at creating the life of my dreams by simply thinking it into reality! What fun! It became crystal clear that the Divine Source (aka: God, the universe, etc.) is not separate and outside of me; it is in fact inside, and accessible to me every minute of every day - all that's required is to believe it and tap into it.

This led me into a voracious reading regimen that was all coming into alignment with my new and improved way of living life. In his book "Manifesting Change: It Couldn't Be Easier", Mike Dooley suggests that life is not a series of random circumstances, but is a direct reflection of our very own thoughts and beliefs. Moreover, spending time, effort, and worry on figuring out "how" to bring about a certain outcome in life is pointless and not our responsibility.

In other words, the process for bringing my desires to fruition is actually none of my damn business! My only responsibility is to dream up my greatest desires, start moving in the general direction of those desires, then watch how God waves His magic wand to turn those dreams into reality. Poof!

Ok, let's take a pause here. If you're asking yourself, "Can living a life full of self-proclaimed bliss really be this easy? Just think up a vision, stick it to my wall, take some action, and watch the miracles unfold?" Well, you're not alone, because I was asking myself the same darn thing! Here I was…a stripper, turned nurse, turned network marketer; and now I'm dreaming up a whole new Casey simply by visualizing it?! Although this initially sounded utterly ridiculous to me, I reached down where that old courage and ambition has always sat inside of me, and I made the decision to give it a shot. And boy has it ever paid off!

One perfect example of visioning has resulted in these very words that you happen to be reading right now! Allow me to explain. After seeing one of my mentor's goal lists, I decided to follow suit by pinning the words "Best Selling Author" to my own vision board. In the moment, this notion seemed ludicrous, as writing was never one of my strongest fortes. However, I held tight to what I had learned about not being responsible for "how" this desired outcome would happen, and concerned myself only with committing fully to my desire of the vision. Most people have heard and understand the idea of "six degrees of separation": this person knew that person, who introduced them to another person, whose grandmother's neighbor knew this person…you get the gist. Well, in this case, there were not only six, but eight degrees which led me to the beautiful beaches of Bali, Indonesia, where I then connected with John Spender, who in turn asked me to share my story for his upcoming book! In the old days, I would have simply chalked this up to a bunch of unfathomable coincidences that happened to lead to a lucky break. But through a great deal of study and practical application, my new Self has been awakened to the magic hand of God that omnisciently weaves together the perfect web of people, places, and things to fulfill our every desire. When we are open to relinquishing the stress and worry of "how" to fulfill our dreams and focus solely on the outcome, we are able to sit back and be observers of the true miracles that unfold through the dance of co-creating a life with God as our partner. I believe that these intricate details of the "how" are without a doubt, the magic of life.

It is nothing short of amazing how the right people will continue to show up and organize around us in a way that is purely bliss, all the while revealing that all things are indeed possible. This idea isn't just wishful thinking, it happens to be a scientific fact. In his incredible work "A Happy Pocket Full of Money", my friend David Cameron Gikandi breaks down the quantum physics behind our ability to attract wealth, abundance, joy, and everything that we desire. This eye-opening book has massively impacted my income, my personal relationships, and my overall outlook on how to live a meaningful, successful life beyond description, and I would not be where I am today without it. I have received countless life-altering gifts through adopting this fairly simple process of what I refer to as "going from closed to open", as I know that you will too.

Seeing the Light

A few vision boards, books, and retreats later, I found myself pivoting toward an even deeper spiritual journey that my soul had begun to crave. Spending more and more time with my spiritual mentors, I became aware of the need to "let go" of trying to solidify an identity of my Self (from my ego's point of view), and focus my thoughts and efforts on unraveling who I really am as a spirit being. I learned how to meditate, how to connect with my higher self, and the importance of how to breathe. In fact, it was during one of these breathing/meditation sessions at a personal development retreat that the most miraculous experience of my life happened: I saw GOD. Seeing God can be explained in many different ways, as every experience is unique; however, I've found that no matter what the details of the story are, finding the words to express to others what it was actually like carries the same degree of difficulty across the board. What does seem to be a common theme is that there is a peacefulness that settles into your soul, incomparable to anything else. Since that retreat, I have placed great importance on studying and applying all of the Universal Laws to my own life, which has resulted in the ability to manifest my desires and turn dreams into reality in unparalleled ways.

Another one of the most influential books that I've read in this realm is "Working with the Law" by Raymond Holliwell. He too has led me to teach these universal principles to those who are searching for their life's purpose and living life to its fullest potential, which has in turn become one of my greatest joys and life-altering gifts that I could ever share.

Love isn't love until you give it away.

In "The Strangest Secret", the great Earl Nightingale addresses how we perceive success in our society, and he quotes psychiatrist and author Rollo May who wrote that "The opposite of courage in our society isn't cowardice - it is conformity." He goes on to explain that this issue of conformity is the primary reason for why there are so many "failed lives" today. Everyone is "acting and behaving like everyone else, without knowing why or without knowing where they are going." The Lord knows, I've had plenty of experience with conforming in order to please others. I believe that one of our greatest desires in life is to feel like we are a part of something - to "belong"; therefore, we conform. Whether consciously or unconsciously, we tend to model what we see. We copy. We mimic. We follow suit.

From an early age, we hear our parents tell us "you can be anything and do anything that you put your mind to"; yet at the very same time, we are instructed and directed to act out a certain cookie-cutter life story. I'm sure it's a story that you've heard before: "Go to school, get good grades, go to college, get a stable job, get married, have a few children, work for 40 years, and save up in your 401K plan for a nice retirement that you might just be fortunate enough to enjoy when you turn 65. We're given the permission to dream as a young child, only to have those dreams take a crushing blow by the so-called "real world". Sound familiar? Too many people have conformed to society's standard of what makes a good life, rather than soul searching to uncover their own.

Living life according to other people's agenda is not really living at all - it's simply existing. I fell into this trap over and over - from wanting to be in the "in crowd" as a youngster, going to college, becoming a nurse, etc.,...but whose dreams was I really following? I've discovered that we will come across many people in our lives, and it's critical to discern which of those people are worthy of following, and which are not.

There is a saying, "Show me who you run with and I'll show you your life." Similarly, I've heard it said that you are the equivalent of the sum of the five people you spend the most time with. I couldn't agree more with both of these statements. As I began to carefully identify the people in my life who were indeed worthy of following because of their core values and how they lived their lives to attract unlimited abundance, I noticed that all the wrong people began to simultaneously fall out of my life and were replaced with all the right people. I made a conscious decision to begin choosing to read the right books, attend the right events, and follow the right people. No longer would I fall into the snare of living my life according to what society OR ANYBODY ELSE suggested. I was on the right path to living the life of my dreams on my own terms, and loving my (spirit) self for finding the courage to step out of conformity and into my own passion and purpose. I was in the process of letting go of my old self so that I might actually find a new self that was worth holding onto.

So now what?? I was earning increasingly more money and becoming what I believed was a pretty darn good successful Network Marketer, and someone who others could trust and follow. But knowing how to lead requires a completely different set of tools, the most important of which comes from the heart. It has been explained to me that you will know a true leader, not by his own success, but by the success of those who are following him. How much are we acting in service to help those people around us? My personal mentors, as well as countless world-class leaders in the realm of personal development are all shining examples of living lives of service and giving their love away. Sharing their knowledge, their experiences and their loving kindness with as many people who have their ears open to listen is how they're changing the world. After all, isn't that the goal of why we're all here?

We all have special God-given gifts inside of us that are just itching for us to unleash onto the world, but conforming to living our lives the way that someone else wants will only smother those gifts until we no longer even know what they are. The greatest leaders don't go looking for people to follow them; instead, they lead by being a real-life example and constantly look for ways to be of service to others through the use of their gifts and talents.

My favorite quote is, "be the change you wish to see in the world." Change! What a beautiful word. It welcomes new possibilities with outstretched arms. If I had not been open to continuously changing careers I might still be swinging around on a pole or picking up overtime shifts in a hospital instead of traveling the world and blessing people with the gift of health and wealth. One thing I'm clear on, is that I continue to move FORWARD in my life because of the aggressive and enthusiastic way that I choose to approach change. What do you love to do? Are you doing it or are you holding your self back and playing it safe? Stay ambitious and open until you find what YOU LOVE to do - trust me, it's so worth it!

Another life-changing principle to mention is that of gratitude. How often are you present in the state of gratitude? Do you even realize and express appreciation for all of the blessings that you've been given? I remember one day that I was griping about doing dishes, while looking down at all of the uneaten food in the trash can and the clean water flowing from the faucet. In an instant, I began to cry. I was shifting into PRESENT MOMENT gratitude. And that's when I recall that the floodgates of abundance really started to open for me.

It would be easy for me to choose to walk around in guilt or shame of my past as a stripper instead of choosing to drum up the courage to overcome it. But I would not be writing these words right now without having experienced that necessary part of my life. I needed that part of my life to happen. Because if it hadn't, an acquaintance wouldn't have introduced me to my friend Jen, who in turn introduced me to network marketing and the greatest nutritional products on the planet. I can choose to be resentful of some not so great choices that I've made, or I can choose to be grateful for the outcome of blessings that were a direct result of those choices.

So here's the advice that I've followed myself and will gladly offer to you: Release the past. Forgive it. Do not only forgive it, but be grateful for it; as every lesson comes with a blessing and is a stepping stone toward your ultimate success. With acceptance of all things comes the reward of inner peace. And in this peace, we have the ability to co-create a fulfilled life with our whole hearts. And when we are in a co-creating partnership with God, all things are possible! We can never go wrong when we are leading with love and listening to the divine spirit that is within every one of us; and this is the voice that attracts unlimited freedom and abundance into our lives.

I'll wrap up with one of my favorite quotes: "It ain't WHAT you know…it's what you THINK you know that just ain't so." Are you harboring your own "WHAT IF?" WHAT IF the ideas that you were once closed off to and KNEW could not possibly be true, actually WERE? WHAT IF an infinite supply of peace, gratitude, happiness, joy, abundance, rich relationships, and prosperous living were offered as a stone-cold promise? Would you be open to changing your mind? Are you open to receiving the many gifts that come along with embracing change and a new perspective? I would like to challenge you right here and right now to write out how you see your dream life with no limits. Write out the physical, the relational, the financial, and the spiritual changes that you desire in your life. Then, on a daily basis, make the time to look at what you've written. Feel it. Touch it. Taste it. Embody it. Spend time doing this visualization exercise, and lovingly monitor the words and thoughts that you speak into your self and into others. In doing this, you are sure to give birth to a mind-blowing transformation.

I wholeheartedly encourage you to make the decision to become the leader of your own parade. Debunk the status quo. You are an extraordinary piece of God's hand-made work! You no longer have to follow past paradigms, conform, or settle for anything less than your wildest dreams. You have permission to go beyond that what you once thought possible. And most importantly, beyond everything else, you have permission to let your old Self go, so that your new Self can "GO!" The true riches of joy, abundance, and peace are not things to be acquired; rather, they are already inside of you, just waiting to blossom.

A dear friend once told me that "it's not who you know, but who you meet along the way" that will open new doors. If you are interested in sharing your journey to love and enlightenment, let's connect! You can find me at casey@caseyplouffe.com or www.FB.com/caseyplouffelive, and be sure to reference this book in your message. From the bottom of my heart, I wish you a magical and transformational ride!

Chapter 3

Forgiveness Is Power

By Marcia Miatke

Every superhero has an origin story. So do you. Don't follow someone else's. Create your own masterpiece

~ Oliver Uberti

When I wake up in the morning and look around my room, I'm sometimes overcome by gratitude for the life I am living. Even now there are days I'm brought to tears when I think about how blessed I am. The fact that I live in a beautiful home in a safe neighbourhood, in country full of opportunity never gets old to me. You see, the life I was born into is worlds apart from the life I live now, and my journey made more beautiful by both incredible highs and agonising lows.

I was born in the remote mountain town of Pampas Peru on December 14, 1984, the fourth child of five. I don't remember much about my life in Peru except that we were very poor. I remember walking up the steep mountainside to a running stream, cupping the water in my hands, and having a drink. I also remember my mother breaking small round bread rolls into pieces so the whole family could eat. At five years old, with no point of comparison, this seemed normal and I remember being happy.

But the walls of our humble home hid our family pain. My father was an alcoholic who was rarely there and when he came home in a drunken state, would beat my mother in front of us. At times he'd turn his anger towards his children. I don't remember much about my father but I have flashes of memory of his anger and violence. Worn down and with little resources, my mother decided that she was unable to take care of all her children. As a result, both my older sister Yadira (Dee) and I were put up for adoption.

In 1990 an incredibly loving, wise and present woman adopted us. She travelled to Peru and spent several months in Lima with us before travelling to Canada to start our new life. I can only imagine the courage it took, as a single woman, to travel to a new country to adopt and commit to raising two children from a different culture and language. For that act alone, she is my hero.

I don't remember the moment I last saw my birth mother and other siblings, or the first time I saw my 'mom'. Years later my mom would describe the day she picked us up from the courthouse where she met our birth mother. I'm sure the first few months in a foreign country with a new mother was a confronting transition period for two small girls but I generally didn't think about my adoption. It wasn't something I consciously reflected on. I often forgot my mom wasn't my biological mother until someone who asked how I felt about being adopted, and whether I ever wanted to see my 'real' family again reminded me. My childhood friends were understandably curious, but sensing it was a sensitive topic, I'm sure asked fewer questions than they wanted.

By all accounts I had a really happy childhood full of positive memories. My happiest memories though were with my big sister Dee, singing, dancing, and laughing. Every day we found a reason to laugh hysterically together. We are still like that, and when we laugh, it's always really loud. I think the reason our best memories are from our childhood is because children live completely in the present. They allow themselves to fully love the moment, regardless of how uneventful it may be, and my childhood was a perfect example of that. Children are our greatest teachers because they have not been disconnected with Source. Their innocence means they inherently know they are magnificent.

While we were busy being kids, my mom worked incredibly hard to give us the best life she could. Though, without a doubt the greatest gift was her uncompromising presence and wisdom, a constant source of peace and strength in our home. Through the years she would teach me the meaning of unconditional love.

It wasn't until high school that I began to think about my adoption more frequently. Although I had so many questions I didn't talk to anyone about them. I thought my sister was the only person who could understand the questions I had and emotions I was feeling. However, unlike me, who had fragmented memories, she had vivid and traumatising memories of our father. It didn't seem fair to bring up old pain since she seemed to be thriving in her new environment, so I buried my feelings. I don't think I was consciously aware of it, but I was becoming increasingly unhappy.

Looking back, I can see that I was angry but like most people, I was conditioned to think that feeling angry was wrong and that expressing anger, especially as a girl, was worse. It would be years of suppressed anger followed by a lot of personal exploration, development and finally self-acceptance before I would come to understand the value in all emotions. In truth, our emotions are messengers; they indicate to us whether what we are thinking about is in line with what we want. Therefore, instead of pushing them away, we should ask, what is this emotion telling me?

The more I buried my feelings, the more I felt ashamed and the lower my self-confidence became. I couldn't shake this sense of unworthiness, and my external world began to reflect this mindset. As I walked into my final year English class the teacher asked me if I was in the right room. I said I was. He pointed out that this was the 'advanced' English class and that I would struggle because English was my second language. My classmates looked on in discomfort as he suggested I switch into an easier class. I remember feeling embarrassed and not knowing how to respond. English was the one class I felt confident in and now I was being told I wasn't good enough to join.

This was just one example of how I was judged for my past and because my confidence was already low, it was experiences like this that stayed with me. I allowed the voices on the outside to be louder than my inner voice. I began to question my abilities and started believing other people's negative perceptions of me.

By the end of high school I was feeling anger and at times, rage, but by this time I was beginning to express it. In fact I was looking for opportunities to let it out. I regularly fought with my mom and sister, who were rightfully concerned about my partying all night, and hanging around the wrong people.

It was during this time that I became friends with other Hispanic people that I met partying. Even though I no longer understood the language or the culture, there was a sense of familiarity because they looked like me. I really wanted to fit in with whom I considered 'my people'. And although I connected with them on some level, many were quick to point out that I wasn't like them, that I was 'white washed.' I wasn't white but I wasn't a true Hispanic either. I was somewhere in between.

I agree with the saying that, "you are the average of the five people you spend most of you're time with". You can either be lifted up or dragged down by your associations. I so badly wanted to feel like I belonged that I started lowering my standards to match that of my friends. I started doing drugs, fighting in clubs, not going to work and rarely coming home. One night frustrated and visibly distressed by my behaviour; my mom asked me if I had given up on life. I remember her question paused my tears and anger. I couldn't answer the question, because I genuinely didn't know.

In 2004 my sister moved to Australia to start University, followed by my mom in 2006 who wanted to migrate back to her country of birth. Afraid to start over again, I decided to stay in Canada. When my family left my already destructive lifestyle got worse. I started using more drugs and alcohol than ever before and became involved in toxic and abusive relationships. I distanced myself from my family and those that truly cared about me and immersed myself in this negative environment.

Despite how bad things had become I was in denial about my lifestyle because I compared myself to my friends who I thought were worse off than me, such as those in extremely abusive relationships or whose bodies needed drugs to physically get out of bed. I remember secretly judging them and thinking - How did you allow your life to become this bad? Why can't you see you're worth more than this? I often gave them advice, which of course they didn't take. I was in no position to give anyone advice about making better life choices. How could I help them when I didn't know how to help myself?

The amount of drugs I took gradually increased until early one morning after a full night of partying my body said no. I was lying in bed and my whole body was frozen. My brain was shouting at my body to move, but it couldn't. There I lay, in an apartment I shared with a heroin addict, away from anyone who genuinely cared about me, unable to move or call for help. I thought this was the end.

Terrified, with tears streaming down my face and onto my neck, I remember thinking, what have I done? How did I get here? My thoughts immediately turned to my mom. I thought about how much she sacrificed to give me the best chance at life, how she worked 12-hour shifts and nights so I could go to a good school, and here I was throwing away everything she worked so hard to give me. I thought about how the news would break her heart. I lay there scared, remorseful and physically frozen, and all I could think about was my mom's love. I couldn't do this to her.

I prayed to God asking for another chance. I prayed out loud begging "Please Lord let me live and I promise I will change my life". My neck and pillow soaked in tears, the last thing I remember before finally closing my eyes was crying please over and over again.

The light at the end of the tunnel is not an illusion. The tunnel is.

The sun came through the window to the left of the bed and shone in my eye. It was so radiant and beautiful. I felt like I was seeing it in its fullness for the first time, which filled me with so much gratitude. I promised my life would never be the same again. And this was a promise I knew I would keep.

It took me hitting rock bottom to finally wake up to the fact that I was destroying my life. That if I continued on this path that I may not survive and if I did, I would feel so trapped that I'd never be able to break free from it. It would become my identity. I couldn't let that happen because despite everything I had been through, I knew this shell of a person that I had become, wasn't me.

If there's no action, you haven't truly decided

~ Tony Robbins

I recognised that completely changing my lifestyle wouldn't be easy and that I would need love and support from my family. After much hesitation I bought a one-way ticket to Australia and called my mom to let her know I was coming to live with her.

After I arrived in Australia my sister encouraged me to apply for university. Although I was unsure I decided to take her advice and applied and was accepted as a mature age student. I was quickly confronted by the difficult transition from a life of excessive partying to being a full-time student for the first time in years. My first semester of business school was particularly challenging and I was constantly pushing away feelings of self-doubt, that I wasn't smart enough and that I didn't belong there. My heart began to race every time I couldn't grasp the concepts discussed in lectures.

I found the whole experience overwhelming as I struggled with theories that other students learned in high school. The fact that I failed both grade ten maths and science kept replaying in my mind. As I sat in my first economics class the lecturer announced, "One quarter of you will fail this unit", I remember being sure he was talking to me. The self-doubt was palpable.

Several weeks into the semester, completely exhausted and frustrated, I broke down to my mom and sister, yelling, "I can't do this, I'm so behind and I keep reading the text book but I still don't get it!" I continued my rant, "I don't know anyone here. I miss my friends. I don't want to be here anymore!"

I shouted and gasped for air as tears flooded my face. I was having an anxiety attack. With so much compassion they hugged me, and my sister said, "We know you are not happy. We know you are struggling and as much as we want you to stay, if you want to go back, we will support you."

I was stunned. My tears immediately disappeared and my panic attack began to subside. I couldn't believe what I was hearing. I couldn't believe they were letting me quit and that they were OK with me going back to Canada, to that horrible life. I said to them silently – "It's because you don't believe in me. You don't think I can do this. Well I can."

If you want something you've never had, you must be willing to do something you've never done

~ Thomas Jefferson

After that conversation I became obsessed with my studies because I was determined to prove them wrong. But my motivation quickly changed when I started to really enjoy the learning process. What began with materials for my classes then expanded to include books on personal development, spirituality, leadership, and success. I also began attending all conferences and seminars I could afford. I knew the fundamental truth that if I wanted more out of life I needed to become more. I whispered to myself: 'I must go within, or I will go without' – which to me meant that I needed to grow as a person if I wanted to achieve success on the outside.

Every day as soon as I got home I jumped into bed surrounded by personal development books and made notes on the points that resonated with me most. I literally fell asleep on my books. Each morning I'd wake up excited to do it again. I loved discussing and analysing the concepts I had learned. My mind had never been so stimulated and I had never felt so alive. I knew I was on to something – I knew I was finding my purpose.

After completing my business degrees I landed an amazing job with an awesome high-performing team at a University. I was so grateful for the opportunity that I consistently came early and left late and put all my energy into doing the best job I could. Within a short time I formed authentic relationships and received incredible professional development and promotions. I had finally reached a point where my external world matched my internal world in the most positive way. I had created a life I really loved.

However, in 2014 my heart told me it was time to make another significant change. After much consideration I decided leave my job to pursue my dream of earning my PhD as well as starting my own business. It wasn't an easy decision, as I enjoyed my challenging and dynamic work, not to mention that my career was going from strength to strength with a pay check to match. Despite the temptation of stick to what seemed stable and secure, I decided to bet on myself. I reminded myself that the price of stability is often fewer opportunities for growth. Although the risks were certainly great, I knew the potential rewards were even greater.

Today that's what I'm doing, following my passion through my PhD research, teaching business at the University and spending time with my family. On December 1st 2015 I gave birth to my baby girl Aliyah Nawal who has already become my greatest blessing and teacher. More broadly, my ultimate life vision is to leave a legacy of love and inspiration both through my work and by how I live my life. By creating from a place of love I intend to contribute to the level of consciousness in the Universe.

Summary

Forgiveness gives you power

We cannot move forward or create lasting change if we are still holding on to hurt from the past. We are taught as children to forgive others because it's the right thing to do. I also learned that people who trigger us to feel negative emotions play an important role in our journey. They are messengers pointing us to the unhealed parts of our being. In our relationships, especially those that are challenging, we should ask, what unresolved pain is this person bringing to the surface? When I was going through my healing phase I thought about the people that hurt me and sent love and forgiveness to them. It was a freeing experience and I felt at peace.

Then one day after I was well settled in my new life in Australia, I decided to open up to my sister about my feelings of being put up for adoption. I asked her "Why us? Our mother had five children, why were the two of us given away?" Feeling the pain resurface, I began to cry, "I was so small, what could I have done to make her want to give me up?" My sister with her innate wisdom didn't let me delve further into my pain, instead she responded, "Then you need to forgive yourself for being put up for adoption."

Her response surprised me, I never considered forgiving myself. I didn't think that I blamed myself for my adoption but I knew I wasn't at peace with it either. Instead of trying to dissect what the unease meant, I put my energy towards forgiving and loving myself. Of course my sister wasn't suggesting that it was our fault, but she recognised the importance of removing the emotional resistance in order to move forward.

Sharing my story is part of my personal forgiveness. It is also the reason I decided to share my whole story rather than just the parts I'm proud of.

By forgiving myself and sharing my story, I hope to inspire others to forgive themselves as well. I believe that when you're authentic, you create space for others to do the same.

The first step to forgiveness is acknowledging the pain. There is no point pretending pain or anger doesn't exist. We need to acknowledge how we feel and be compassionate towards ourselves. Once you stop making a negative emotion wrong, it's easier to let it go. Only then can you tap into your true power, which allows you to release fear, heal old wounds and stop playing the victim. As Socrates so accurately stated, 'Change is not about fighting the old but creating the new.' Holding on to old grievances whether towards someone else or to oneself takes up a great amount of energy, energy that could be redirected to creating the new. Forgiveness truly sets you free and without it you are bound to repeat old patterns. True forgiveness is saying 'thank you for the experience.' How many people can you thank for contributing to the person you are today?

Your past doesn't equal your future

If I continued to believe that my past equals my future then I would still be a little orphan girl or a drug addict on the inside. Neither of those are who I am today. The reason I don't identify with either of those is simply because I choose not to. We get to choose who we are in this life by the meaning we give our experiences. Shakespeare said it best when he concluded, 'Nothing is good or bad, but thinking makes it so.' This statement highlights, the fundamental truth that the only meaning anything has is the meaning we give to it. Instead of being ashamed or embarrassed of my past, I look to it for strength and wisdom. I ask myself, what has being adopted taught me about giving more love and compassion to others? How can I transform the pain I experienced through drug use into something meaningful?

We literally create our reality by how we choose to perceive things. That's why I choose to see all my past experiences as gifts, regardless of how painful they may have been in the moment. A little time and perspective can go a long way in the healing process. Instead of being upset by a 'negative' experience, try to use it as a point of contrast that allows you to get incredibly clear about what you do want. For example, my experience of hitting rock bottom helped me to get very specific and then set strong intentions about my ideal lifestyle. Now when I am going through a challenging period I try to remind myself 'New beginnings are often disguised as painful endings.' We must remember that incredible gifts can come packaged in pain, failure, fear or loss. Take a moment to think about what beautiful gifts your past has blessed you with.

You are capable of transformational change

Regardless of where you are in your life, you are capable of transformational change. It isn't that some people are able to change and others are not, I believe that some are ready to change while others are not. If you are not truly ready and willing to change, no approach or strategy will get and keep you where you want to be. For instance, when I hit rock bottom, I was both ready and willing to transform my life. It wasn't something I kind of wanted; my mind was made up and there was no alternative. First decide you want to change and then take immediate action. When your goal is definite, any obstacle, excuse and limitation can be overcome.

It's also important to understand that our emotions are an incredibly powerful resources to achieve our goals. When we learn to master them we can use them to our benefit. When I decided to attend university as a mature age student, I was afraid of stepping out of my comfort zone. Instead of being consumed by fear as I had in the past, I began imagining how my quality of life would be improved after I earned my degree. I allowed myself to feel the joy I would feel when I could finally give back financially to my mom, as gratitude for all she had done for me. In unison, I allowed myself to tap into the pain I felt when I wasn't able to provide for myself and the poor decisions I made when I thought I didn't have better choices. In that instance I associated more pain with the status quo than my fear of starting something new.

Moreover, people often see fear as a weakness but this isn't so. Fear is only a problem when it paralyses you from moving forward. It's how you perceive your fear that impacts your ability to overcome it. If you begin to view your fear as an opportunity for growth you feel empowered rather than helpless. Remember courage does not exist in the absence of fear, and to be courageous there must be an element of apprehension. If there is something you want to do but you are afraid, acknowledge and move towards it and in so doing, you will transcend it.

My story underscores the universal truth that change is the only thing we can be certain of in this life. And that based on our perception it can feel like synchronicity and flow or like struggle. The incredible Robin Sharma so succinctly describes the process of change 'Change is hard at first, messy in the middle and beautiful at the end.' I couldn't agree more. At times change can be hard and it can get messy too, but in the end, the beauty he promises is the person you become as a result of it.

Chapter 4

Awaken to Your Magnificence and the Magic All Around You

By John Abbott

The story starts like many stories, an eager young man, keen to impress by creating success for himself and his family.

And for him, this is the part of a journey of understanding who he really was.

You know those times in your life when everything just seems to keep going right, like nothing you do can go wrong?

Well that's not this story, this story is the one that happens just after that story.

Let me take a moment to go back in time, back when it was all going just 'swimmingly'. Picture this, 2008, you're in Australia and the property and mining boom are at the very peak, actually some would argue that it was past it's peak. Six years of this growth, and in 2007, we could not make a mistake in property. Buy today at an inflated price and put it back on the market the next week and profit $40-50k. So as you do, I decided to buy six of them, land to be subdivided into twelve, which we did, however come 2009, we were caught holding this stock that had dropped 25 to 30 percent. So now we're in serious trouble, purchased to high and I had to find a way to exit this project in a hurry.

During the same time I'd decided to open a shared office and conferencing centre. I got the building I wanted, I paid premium rent, and again in less than a few months after we opened the GFC had an interesting impact on my 'not so prudent' investment decision. A year after opening we had to shut the doors. It's kind of weird, life was looking so good. I had a few good wins, and for a moment you think to yourself "nothing can go wrong" and at the same time you've got this feeling in your gut, a little voice in your head saying "watch yourself". You then find yourself expecting, feeling and looking for signs to support your doubt. Of course life goes in ebbs and flows and just like the surfer rides the waves, when the wave ends you have to get back on board and paddle out.

In 2006 - 2007, when I was riding this wave, I felt almost invincible, loving life, everything seemed to be flowing, doing some great projects with good people. Totally oblivious of the depths of debt I was in, well maybe not oblivious of it, but just not looking at the potential risks at all, thinking, I'm going to ride this wave for ever. The point of this is I hadn't done the work that you really need to do and I didn't consider what the ramifications would be if it went wrong. I didn't have that backup insurance plan. I hadn't taken the time to set it all in place, I was caught up in the ego of 'over indulging' in the buffet that was laid out in front of me.

The signs were there, and I was being warned with little things, the little voice in the back of my head telling me to slow it all down. Let me say, if you decide to ignore these little signs, these whispers, they only get louder. The signs came as a bunch of bills and salaries that I had no idea how to pay. It was tens of thousands of Dollars, and as much as I'd been avoiding them and postponing and "stealing from Peter to pay Paul" i.e. pulling money out of my personal savings, it was now that big and my well had run so dry that I had no option but to stop… And at that moment I realized what a nightmare I had created, a train smash really, and I had put my family in jeopardy. I had nothing left in me, I couldn't put another paddle stroke in… I found myself in a place of disbelief, depression and was questioning my own sanity.

It's times like these that we either loose ourselves and spiral into a state of depression and guilt, or we're ready for the lessons and from a place of understanding and humility, we discover ourselves. In my case, I was not there yet, I was questioning what the hell just happened, blaming myself, coming down on myself so hard, given it was 'all my fault'. We are always going to be harder on ourselves than anyone else can be. My suggestion to you in hindsight is, be gentle on yourself.

I was questioning, what had just happened, in disbelief of what my world had become, and how careless I'd been. Some of the hardest stuff I was dealing with was the people who were involved, the people who had invested in me, the people who had given their time and money, belief and trust. Our team, the people who had been showing up each day giving their all to help make this a success, who all had rents and mortgages and expenses to pay, and were relying on me.

I now needed to give them the bad news.

I needed to deal with their disappointment, their judgement and potentially anger and backlash. It was a massive challenge letting them go and hoping that they'd be okay ... I felt so much guilt. In some of our businesses we'd sold shares to investors, and the big part of this was the trust they had put in me to create a return for their investment. I felt responsible for their loss, for inviting them in and putting them at risk. Could I have foreseen, could I had gotten better advice, had my ear to the ground, could I have predicted the impact of the GFC. I had a lot of stuff going on about this, considering that there were signs that I could have responded quicker, however like many, I was caught up in the wave and the excitement and caught up in the possibilities. To be totally honest, I simply didn't want it to finish, and hence was ignoring anything that indicated it was over.

The ego is strong in this one

A lot of the reasons for us not hearing or seeing the warning signs or not responding to the signs especially when things seem to be going right is that our ego is in control and running its racket in our mind.

The ego was very much in control with me, convincing me this was not over, and of course doing its duty, the duty of keeping me safe in what it felt was a good situation. The status of having nice cars, living in affluent areas and being the head of high level networks was all feeding the ego, and the ego was loving the attention.

Sometimes our ego can get so strong that even when we get the opportunity to receive a learning, to get out of ego, stop and look around and make a better decision, the ego simply overrules and suppresses our ability to listen. The ego was totally running my show, and although there were many, many signs for me to stop doing all those things I was doing that was sabotaging my life. I couldn't see them, it really didn't matter if you or 100 people had told me to pull out of the investments I was getting myself into or to make different decisions and commitments I was making. I had all the answers and could justify every part of it, even if I had to convince myself.

I'd gone to professionals to get advice on smart investment strategies, structures and how to keep myself personally safe with contracts or commitments, and although I'd done some of them, I was just reckless, signing personal liability for financial risks. So although all of that was there, and it looked like I was doing the work, if I felt I needed to shortcut the process to make something happen faster, I did. The signs were certainly there and the more I put myself at risk, the more signs showed up for me, and I was choosing not to hear them.

The biggest of all these signs came from my wife. She could see it all because she wasn't attached, she wasn't emotionally bought in, like I was.

And with the level of my buy-in, I didn't want to let it go either. I wanted to keep all of them going, I wanted to keep the investments, wanted to save the conference centre, hold onto our IT company, however, as it was, all of them were to come to an end, with or without me. My wife, although she stood by my side all the way through this, with all my justifying and ignoring of her warning bells, she decided to make a stand and served me with the ultimate warning. It truly was the final straw for her, and the one that needed to be dealt to me to essentially wake me up.

The universe always gives us a heads up

The universe is wonderful like that, it gives us a number of messages and if you don't get the messages and make better decisions, it cranks up the intensity of the message, turns up the volume and eventually screams at you. No matter how much you decide to ignore them, hold onto the past or things that are no longer serving your greatest self, the end result if you choose not to listen is that you'll end up loosing. That's just the way it is, and in reflection a big part of our life success is in us stopping and listening to those whispers and knowing that the messages are always there. And if we can, even for just a moment, quieten our ego for long enough to see and hear the truth of who we really are, then these whispers start to become more prominent, they become loud flashing red, orange and green lights that we can trust to assist us to make much better decisions for our lives.

It had gotten to a point where I was on a call to my mentor, and he was screaming down the phone to me saying "John if you don't let this go and stop trying to be the hero, you are going to not only lose me as your mentor but you are also going to lose your family".

That reality check, dealt at the same time as my wife's, really closed the deal for me. Just the thought of loosing my family, my wife, the thought that she's going to leave me, suddenly I realised that I'd been pushing her away, having arguments where I was taking a high road, saying "you know I am personally liable for these debts, I've created this mess, I will sort it out, I will pay them back, I will handle this". Of course that was all utter rubbish, and just listen to the egoic voice in that language. At the end of the day we create businesses and structures to limit our liability, hence the 3 letters after the company name Ltd. We never have to put ourselves and our families in danger, and as long as our intentions are true and we do everything in our power to act to the best of our ability, then that's our primary responsibility.

Of course there were a few things I was personally responsible for, and there may be good reason for you to pay certain loans back if you find yourself in a position like this, however if you find yourself taking the high road and holding on to a story that has you 'be the hero', saving people, 'doing the right thing' even when you're not commercially liable, then that's a clue that the ego is in control. After that conversation I decided to shut down the businesses, I stopped trying to solve the problems and I went to a place of acceptance.

Holding on only causes greater tension

Holding on so tightly had caused everything to come crashing down, and one by one I had to deal with them. There are always 2 ways to respond to things crashing down around you, either you can go into denial and blame and take no responsibility for any of it, and potentially miss the learning, or you can decide to surrender, acknowledge that you messed up, and ask yourself better questions like;

> When did I first get the messages? (So you can be more conscious when you see them again)

> What could I have done differently? (Being clear of what a better decision looks like)

Who are the people who have stood with me all the way through? (Knowing who your real friends are)

What am I grateful for from this experience? (Feeling how being grateful can change your state and emotional attachment to the event)

Why was it perfect? (See the perfection in everything that's often hidden until you ask the question)

Solving problems only creates more problems

It was almost a year of me trying to solve the problems of the breakdowns that where happening, the breakdowns in the network that I was running and managing, the breakdowns in the centre that I was running, the breakdowns in the development I had invested in, all the different things I was dealing with personally and the breakdowns in our ability to create enough to service all expenses and debts. And if you'd asked me in those days "are you a good problem solver?" I would say YES, I am a brilliant problem solver, this is the stuff I do every day, I solve problems, no matter what the issue, I'll find a solution and I'll make it work. I'd always been really good at taking broken things and making them work.

The issue with trying to solve problems, is that you create a consistent way of life, attracting more problems for you to solve. For a moment, just get the impact of that, if you are a problem solver right now and one of the things you love to do is solve problems, like anything in life, whatever you focus on grows, if you focus on solving problems you absolutely will find more problems to solve. So if you're looking for a life which is less complicated with less problems and a business that has less problems, then this may well be the one thing you get out of this story.

Now, some people love it and they will continue doing this for the rest of their lives and maybe right now is not the time for you to hear it, however if you're feeling the impact of this in this moment, then it is time to really make a new decision on this and stop solving the problems. Instead create new end results that you want. By this I mean, ask yourself a better, bigger question. Ask a question that you've never considered, one you don't have the answer for, and by doing that, you can't go back to old ways of doing things, you have to connect into your own creativity, your higher self and potential and allow magic to show up to guide you to create a new reality.

"You never change things by fighting the existing reality. To change something, build a new model that makes the existing model obsolete."

~ R. Buckminster Fuller

This insight and process is probably one of the biggest lessons I've learned in my life as it's taken me to places I could not have imagined.

Sitting in the ashes

So often we get caught up in a breakdown, in a business breakdown, in a financial breakdown, in a relationship breakdown, and find ourselves trying to save it. Trying so hard to save a part or aspect of it. What I mean by breakdown is an ending, a completion, I'm not saying giving up when you're in conflict or having a 'bad day'.

As the phoenix rises from the ashes what we so often don't get and what I found so valuable was allowing everything to be destroyed and burned into ashes. And from sitting longer and uncomfortably in these ashes, allowing the ashes to really settle, allowing all the burning embers to die down to become cold coals without any charge, to a place where you know you've moved on emotionally and released the past. Usually this takes about 2-3 times longer than you think. For instance, this last time it took me 4 months of doing nothing on my business, and it really stretched me to resist and be in the moment, to allow all the learnings to really sink in, allow gratefulness to rise and most importantly, allow you to move forward without any of the attachment of the past. This is the part that actually sets the phoenix up to rise into it's full potential and magnificence. So often we're caught up in imagining, visualising and thinking about what the next thing will be, what the phoenix will rise up to be. Being fixated on the phoenix doesn't allow us to complete on the previous journey.

At this stage of my journey I did not understand this, and I grabbed hold of a few things that I thought I needed to keep, that I was familiar with, even though I knew they were not serving me. Five years later and I was still being reminded that they are still there and I had to deal them again at another level. This, all because I hadn't allowed myself to actually complete on them, allow them to totally die out and return to nothing.

Destroy unsupportive structures

Starting with a blank page, I decided to start to rebuild different aspects of my life and business. Tapping into what my core skills are and purpose is, and what there was for me to take to market. I've always been good at sales, been great in consulting roles and working one on one with people on their marketing and sales strategies. I decided that rather than trying to work out where I added most value, I'd simply got out and offer support and gave service to someone else's business, assisted them with marketing, helped them with their events, their presentations, and for the next ten weeks I was able to rebuild and reconnect to myself, to a point where I could see and feel the value I was able to bring to others. It was really a great process, and I didn't have to think about my business, I didn't have to think about accounting and billing, I didn't have to think about hiring a team or staff, all I had to do was give value in service.

So when I got to the end of the ten weeks I decided it was time for me to create my new environment, to do something in my life that was totally outside of what I could imagine. I was also asking for this exact kind of sea change, the exact kind of shift away from what I could see was a system that had been holding me to ransom. So after a discussion, my wife and I decided to leave to Bali, totally excited and a little nervous about what was install for us. And of course what always happens on journeys like these is the most extraordinary things show up, magic seems to just happen and we embarked on a journey that we both could never have planned, expected or contemplated that has changed our lives for ever. More about that another day.

My wife and I ended up living in a resort for the next year and a half, having an amazing time working with the beautiful Balinese people and enjoying the opportunities that were available, finding amazing entrepreneurs to work with and going on physical adventures around the island. We were able to do this without all the noise of what is quite often the bugbear of being an entrepreneur. But like everything in our lives, change is always just around the corner and after we decided to re-establish our business, re-creating our marketing business, inviting people in from around the world to come and join us in Bali, we started creating a team. I had carried out marketing and events promotion for some prominent speakers and trainers in the past and decided to create a program whereby we could attract more people in, add more value and changes lives at a whole new and different level.

At first it came easy, the program came together, people wanted to partner with us and invited their audience to listen in and be part of it, and for the next 6 months we couldn't put a foot wrong, or it felt that way.

Then slowly but surely we started to have to push harder, we worked harder and although we were having a lot of fun their was a part of me that felt we were heading off track. We'd taken the initial idea and it had turned into multiple services, we were hiring more people, we were taking on big projects, and all the while moving further and further away from the original intent. Hence, we were having to push. I had a feeling at this stage that if we stopped pushing hard the whole thing would come crashing down. It got to a stage where I decided to test if this was sustainable, see what would happen if I took my foot off the pedal. And surprise, surprise… What happened was all the different parts of it just started to fail and I realized that it was time to make another change.

With the help of my mentor at that time, I was able to see that the structure I had put in place was no longer serving me and because of that mentorship it allowed me to very quickly shut down and reconsider other options, be able to shift and move to what was the obvious next step. That meant we would unfortunately let some people go, consolidate a few things and identify and focus on what our core business was.

We made a decision on core products, and made a very big decision on who our core clients would be. This may have been one of the biggest and best decisions, defining who our clients where, and also really defining who our clients were not, so that we could really see them clearly from afar. That is the big part of being able to have a business that is sustainable, only working with people you truly love, trust and who you know you can add massive value to.

We defined at what level of the game our clients would be playing, what kind of following they would have, what kind of impact they were having on people through their message, services and products, and what kind of products they would have. This formed part of our client definition and I really would encourage you, if you are an entrepreneur or considering it, if you are not crystal clear on what your client looks like and who your client is not, then make a decision today to define that.

When I made the decision to no longer work with anyone else, even if they had the money, in fact, especially if they just had the money, things started to flow and work so much simpler. If you are not working with the people who are at least 99% your client then you are already starting a relationship for the wrong reasons, so consider that may not be the energy or the kind of frequency of business that you want to be part of.

A practice into being

Everything is perfect all the time. No need to react, no need to blame, no need to look at negative reasons, no need to complain. Everything happens for a reason in the greater scheme of things. Our job is to see the perfection in it, and be grateful for it. This way of thinking and being is some of the biggest challenges I've taken on in my life, and currently I have a "Complaint Free World" wristband that I'm wearing and it's a constant reminder of this very fact, that "Everything is perfect". And as much as it does not look like it in that moment, it's during those times that you really get to see the magic and opportunity in it. Everything is absolutely, meticulously masterminded, perfect in every single way and our job really is to see what that perfection is for us in everything that shows up.

All events are neutral events, we create the meaning based on our beliefs and filters of how we see the world. Life doesn't happen to you, life happens FOR YOU! Become the observer, the witness of your life. When we are able to show up with the attitude that everything is there to support what we truly want in our life, then clearly part of our job is to define what we truly want for our life and tune into that regularly.

Expecting and enjoying the magic

There is magic in every day. There is magic happening all around us, in every moment, and of course, there is magic inside of every one of us. This magic we were born with is there for us to live a life that inspires us, and to shine our light on others. What I do today and in every single moment, in meeting with each challenge, in every opportunity that shows up, is looking for and acknowledging the magic in that. When you wake up expecting magic to show up in your life and looking for evidence of that, I promise you this… What you focus on grows in your life. I promise you'll start to see the magic, you'll start to notice that there are no coincidences, meetings, you'll start to sense the reason why you scan through someones Facebook post and start a conversation, you'll begin to notice the magic that is there. The magic that is happening all the time, but because we have been unconscious to it, unconscious of what we were actually looking at, we could not have seen it before. Be present to this or you'll miss the real magic, that's there all of the time for you. Expect and enjoy the magic of life that is absolutely abundant, absolutely perfect and you now have the opportunity to bathe in its perfection.

Choose an inspiring environment

Freedom!

My definition is this… The choice to live anywhere in the world, in an environment that most supports the lifestyle you've dreamed of and desire for you and your family.

I've had the most extraordinary opportunity to relocate to Bali for over 6 years already. We've been able to create a business, support others building their business and encouraged many of our friends to join us here in Bali. Using all that I've learned along the way, and there is much more to learn, I've been able to mentor other entrepreneurs on how to create global enterprises and create freedom in their own lives. I love family, my friends, the outdoors, sports, travel and thoroughly enjoy business. If you'd like to connect with me further, pop onto www.johnabbott.me and register for one of my free programs, or reach out to me and let me know how this book has impacted you and I'll happily add you to my inner network of friends, colleagues and partners so that you can start to connect with the extraordinary people I get to hang out with too, and who knows, maybe you too will decide to join me in Bali.

Chapter 5

Passion is your Greatest Possession

By Goro Gupta

So I click the paddle to downshift the gear on the $650,000 McLaren supercar and just for a moment time freezes as if I have just entered a meditative state before launching myself and this amazing piece of machinery in the palm of my sweaty hands at the curvy road ahead. In this moment of time freeze, as the adrenaline rushes through my body, life flashes before my eyes – not the kind where one would imagine the end of their life, but more a moment of gratitude for the life that has that brought me to this very moment.

This is my journey of riches and I am Goro Gupta. The greatest possession in my life is my passion!

For the real story behind this journey, I have to go back to a long time ago, even before I was born, in fact, to a time when India was born – for my belief is that true wealth is generational. As the British rule ended in India in 1947, they started a civil war that still continues to this day. During the leaving of the British empire, India was split into three countries, causing the largest mass immigration the world has ever seen. During this time, countries were created on the basis of religion, causing the uprooting of hundreds of thousands of families and violence that one cannot even begin to imagine.

It was during this upheaval that my grandfather (a Hindu) who lived his whole life in what is now known as Pakistan had to make the perilous journey to New Delhi as a refugee. Many in his family perished along the way, including his mother and father. Living in the refugee camp, he married my grandmother, another refugee also from the now known Pakistan. During this time, even as a refugee without a home, he decided that he would not let life decide what he did – so he started a business selling pickles (something he continued till his 60's!). Of course, that action of taking matters into his own hands when he had nothing at all was barely enough to pay the bills, and he couldn't even send all his children to high school. But what that action did was to start a chain reaction that will allow even my grandchildren to live a life of their choosing!

Dad had a dream, it wasn't a large dream as per today's standards, but it was a large dream for the boy that was once told to herd goats because his parents couldn't afford to send him to high school. After getting a scholarship to attend high school and University, his dream was always to leave India for a better life and start his own business. Even though I was born in India, my earliest memories were of the flat we lived in Dubai when I was 4 years old, and I remember times when my family were happy and times when my family were not as happy. I recall that these times were often due to what Mum and Dad called 'money'.

This dream took him to Iraq and then Dubai. In Dubai, Dad had worked with a local 'sheik' (who is now a very wealthy man governing over the finances of a neighbouring state of Dubai). This Sheik had promised him income if Dad took the risk and grew his business as if it was his own. This 'commission' was always 'coming' but never actually appeared – all the while he drove around in the latest Mercedes. The company to this day, using Dad's best practice procedures is the largest company of its kind in the United Arab Emirates. One day when Dad had enough, he stormed into the Sheiks office and threatened court action, at which point in time Dad's passport was seized (common practice still to this day in Dubai!). While it took years and thousands of dollars (a lot of money in the 1980's for a family living on a small income) to get his passport back, one of Dad's friends suggested that he emigrate to this place he had heard of rarely – called Australia.

'Australia is the land of opportunity, and unlike Dubai, you can have your own business there as well!'. This was music to Dad's ears, and he started the process of emigrating to what is now our homeland – all without a passport or a cent to his name.

'Let's pack, we are moving our lives'. Over the next 6 months, we packed up everything we had, ready to move to a country we had never seen before (except on a map).

Somehow, after almost a year of false accusations in court, he managed to get his passport back. He left the country ASAP leaving us behind for a few months, thinking - 'Life will be great in Australia, there are so many jobs out there, an engineer like myself should be able to find one easily.' Life had different ideas however. He landed in Australia just as 'the recession we had to have' started. He applied for hundreds of jobs during this time, all with no luck. But he didn't despair, he mowed lawns on the weekend to try to earn enough to pay the rent as his family was about to arrive.

When we arrived in Australia, I was age 7, I remember all the rolling green hills of Melbourne thinking – wow, this is a new adventure! But as we got out of the airport, I realised that Dad didn't have a car, he instead hired a taxi to get us to our small 2-bedroom apartment. Coming from a country where wealth was splashed around everywhere, I recall thinking – this isn't what I thought it would be like here.

Being a recent immigrant during a recession, it was next to impossible to find a job. My dad didn't have a job and spent all his time either interviewing or gaining skills at what was then known as a Job Club. Conversely, Mum, having PHD in Applied Mathematics managed to get a job at Monash University as a lecturer!

I remember going to my first primary school and not really fitting in (I was new to the country after all!) and all these kids going to 'after school care' – while my parents just told me to go to the library after school. I'm sure my parents did this to save money, but it was this very action that gave me an invaluable foundation for life – where I started reading books of both fiction and non-fiction for hours at the library until my parents got home. I was a voracious book reader and enjoyed them so much I used to take them home with me to read! This laid the principles which I now carry with me -

'Self-education is imperative to live the life you dream of.'

A few months after landing in the country, I found out I was having a baby sister! As Mum was the temporary bread winner in the family, and now pregnant, we had to really clamp down as we had no riches but the richness of our new family in Australia. I recall a moment as clear as day which always drives me to create wealth for my children (which I don't have any of yet!) and their children –

Me: 'Mum, can I go on the school excursion to the aquarium'

Mum: 'How much will it cost?'

Me: '$15'

Mum: '*We can't afford it.*'

I then went to school and told the teacher and my fellow students – 'I am afraid of the sharks, that's why I can't go.'

Mum saying 'We can't afford it' is etched into my brain, and I use that as a platform to help me create wealth not only for myself, but others as well. I never want myself or others to ever be put into that situation. It might sound weird and small, but these 4 words have changed my life where, just like most successful people, I used that pain to drive me and say – NEVER AGAIN! I learnt a valuable lesson that day.

'Don't let pain use you, instead use pain to drive you from the depths that you are in, into the space where you belong.'

Part of this lesson is creating a passive income from a financial security point of view. One of the first few steps of what I ask my coaching clients to do is to get a hold of Tim Ferriss's spreadsheet on what life costs typically are (this is available on his blog) and outline specifically what it would cost them to live their life from a security point of view. I then start the process of helping them achieve financial certainty passively. I find that once we create enough passive income on a monthly level to achieve financial certainty, for some reason, life becomes 'easier' and a fear we all have unconsciously goes away almost immediately. The 'what happens if I lose my job or business'? question turns to –

'What happens if I don't follow my life purpose?'

The formula to live a life of your choosing, of your cause, of your mission is so very simple – find out what it would cost you to get, and create it passively.

Fast forward to when I was 15………

Dad purchased a business where we sold, repaired and maintained cash registers. While this business doesn't seem like much now, imagine in the late 90's – every shop had a cash register! Owning a business was Dads eternal dream ever since University and he had finally achieved it! He was so proud he even brought his family to work in it. Mum left her full time lecturer job at Monash University and worked as accounts receivable, my uncle who emigrated to Australia started working in the technology division. But it was me that got my first lesson in running a business. Dad told me one day –

'Son, in order to run a business, you have to do every single role and understand every job as if it was your own.'

So I started from the bottom of the organisation cleaning cash registers after school and on weekends. After doing this for a while, I got 'promoted' to canvassing. Canvassing was the role of walking into a shop and placing our stickers on cash registers so people would call us if their register broke down. This lead to my second lesson in running a business –

'Never be afraid of talking to potential customers – they need you more than you need them.'

At the age of 16, during my school holidays, I walked shop to shop, interacting with people double my age or more on a daily basis. This taught me how to overcome the fear of talking to people and to find out what they really want in order to give them the solution to their problems.

A year later, while I was at Melbourne High School, I started the touchscreen division of the company and even had 2 employees working under me – all while I was still at school. A division that at one stage had 8 employees. The lessons I learnt in business and in school started merging together as one, and I started implementing the lessons straight away. In fact, due to this, I ended up as one of the top 10 students in the state for my Business Mastery subject. Interestingly my classmate got 1st in the state – who is now the richest man in my age group in Australia, Ruslan Kogan. I learnt a new lesson here –

'There isn't a separation of life and business, there is simply an integration which allows for flow.'

During this time, my dad had an invitation to attend a real estate course by (the now notorious) Henry Kaye. He attended his first ever seminar and he was hooked. He then invested over $50,000 (once again a LOT of money in the late 90's) attending his top level courses. Of course, while most people lost money and claimed they didn't get the results they wanted, I saw Dad purchase 8 properties in under 4 years. During these events, my father invited me to the seminars and I learnt another key lesson –

'Learning something without action is useless.'

It was at this time, after hearing about it at those seminars, I picked up this book called 'Rich Dad, Poor Dad' and started reading it. I was blown away and soon after I turned 18 and was given a gift from my parents – 'With this $30,000, you can either buy the car of your dreams or use this as a deposit on your very first property'. Of course most kids would have picked the car, but after reading the book, how could I not choose the property option? While my friends dreamt of having their dream car, I dreamt of building an empire. It was then I realised I had been given an ever greater gift of another lesson which I ask my clients every day –

'How will the financial action you take right now affect you 5 years on?'

As for the dream car, well that's an interesting story, after driving my parents old Camry for a couple of years, I found a guy that wanted to trade in his sports car for a Camry! It was the perfect car – It was a pearl white V8 Lexus coupe, complete with electric leather seats and a huge sunroof! One day, as it sat in the driveway, I was going through my old computer backup and stumbled upon my old screen saver, and realised that the picture was almost the same as the car I now owned. This was all before The Secret and I learnt another lesson –

'Put it out there, work your ass off and let go of the need to own it, and it will be yours in due time.'

When I was 19, I attended my first Tony Robbins event and just like my parents who had attended the year before – I was hooked. This event was everything I loved and more. I finally found that I was in a room of 4000 people and that I BELONGED here. I found my tribe. As the 4 day fire walk event came to a close – I found that I could attend his 'university'. Of course, all the savings I had was going towards my second property, so I called my parents and borrowed $15,000 from them vowing to pay it back within a year. Not only did I pay them back within 3 months after learning the skills to motivate my staff even more, but it laid the foundation for one of the business's I have now which I run as a result of this lesson

'Successful people don't ask if it can be done, they ask – What needs to happen for me to achieve this outcome?'

After years of running my computerised cash register business, and attending personal development events. I realised something – that my mission in life was greater than selling touch screen and Point of Sale equipment, so I set on the path to selling this business. Once sold, I went to work for a corporate company in Perth selling IT equipment, thinking that working in corporate would be a 'cool idea'. But I was not satisfied at all and realised what a mistake I had made. Of course this led me to my next lesson –

'If you aren't following your mission, your soul will give you the hints you need.'

After this, I left and retired for the first time (at the ripe old age of 25). And went to 'search' for something that was a fit for my meaning in life. At this time I met a man who at that time was 'Australia's Tony

Robbins'. Money not being a concern, I was free to follow a path of my choosing. As I attended my first event with him, I recall going to the presenter at the front of the room and the following conversation occurring –

Me: 'Hey this seems like a cool company, I'd love to work here'

Her: 'We just hired a whole heap of staff, we aren't really looking anymore'

Me: 'Give me a desk and a phone, that's all I need'

Her: 'What do you mean?'

Me: 'I don't need a job, I'll work on commission only and it will be the best decision you have ever made'

Her: 'Can you start next week?'

As I worked there, I rose to the ranks of being the top 'sales-person' and eventually one of the sales managers. From this, I realised a new lesson–

'Life will rarely gift you opportunities, YOU have to create them.'

For years I worked in this company as if it was my own business, following my mission and my path which was to help others create the financial freedom that they deserved. The owner of the business and I became close friends and I started to get close to people who were wealthier than my family and I (at this stage we had about 14 properties). Being around these people scared the hell out of me because I felt for years I was a little fish amongst these big sharks. As time went on, I realised that these people saw me almost as equals even though I didn't believe it at first. Interestingly, along this journey working for this company, I met some people who are very close friends of mine, including John Spender!

Touring the country and speaking on stage with people like Arnold Schwarzenegger, Richard Branson and Tim Ferriss was part of the coolest experiences of my life that I could not have even dreamt of (I still pinch myself to this day!). I even had presenters who I had once learnt from at events ask me for advice on their presentation! One day, on a cruise in the middle of the Caribbean, at about 1am and more than a few cocktails, an astronaut friend said to me – Goro, your better than this, start something new'. A new lesson was in order –

'Play the game with people who scare the hell out of you, for you have more to offer than you know.'

At this same time, Mum and Dad wanted me to work for their finance company, which they had started up after we sold our cash register business over 5 years before. I felt conflicted. I was following my passion, but working for another person – at the same time I knew that doing something with the family would be beneficial. It was then I asked myself –

'How do I bring doing something I love and mix it with family wealth?'

And as I recalled a time when I had to borrow money from my parents to attend my first high end event, I thought to myself - not everyone has parents like mine, but what if they had the access they needed to the funding that would help change their lives? And voila, the company now known as Momentum Education Finance was born.

This company, which now is the largest of its kind in the industry, works with seminars and events in order to get their attendees to create the life change they need in their lives. At that time I recall setting a clear intention, an intention and a goal. That goal was to work with the largest personal development name in the world – Tony Robbins. I am blessed that 2 years ago, this became a reality. I even got to help write some of his script! The lesson I learnt from this was –

'When starting your business, set a clear intention – a goal that scares you. Then do what it takes to get your ass there!'

While creating this business, I realised that this was going to be my nest egg, my cash flow. But I had always wanted this at the same time to be my 'passive income' business. I recall reading Rich Dad, Poor Dad, where Robert Kiyosaki talked about creating a passive income business. So this was my first experiment, where I had to create, innovate and employ the right staff to create financial freedom for myself. This took years and still to this day takes time as its always growing – even though its fairly passive. I learnt a new lesson –

'A passive income business will take years to create, and once created, will still take a little bit of time – there is no such thing as hands off passive. Freedom and choice should be the end result, not passive.'

While setting up this business, working with my parents was challenging. Even after working on myself and my mindset I believed I wasn't truly wealthy or successful. I recall at times putting on the 'clothes' of success, but due to the voices I kept hearing from my parents and others around me, never actually believing this. When I asked my parents – what does success mean to you, I found my parent's version of success was not only a successful company, where I took control of everything, but also being married. I finally gave into this and decided I had to get married. My parents arranged for me to be married (yes, an arranged marriage). Unfortunately, this marriage didn't work out due to various reasons which includes both cultural and financial differences. I learnt quite a few lessons during this difficult time of my life, but the most important one -

'Follow your own path of success and when you achieve it, don't let anyone tell you that you aren't successful.'

After going through a 21-day marriage (yes, that's not a typo), I decided I needed some time to reflect on the things that had happened and retired for the second time in my life. I went and lived in Phuket while having the business run itself. In this time, I discovered one thing – I get bored really quickly. I even recall sharing this story with Tim Ferriss and he then asked me –

'Goro, when you did retire, did you do something with your time? Because the same mindset that got you to retire on the beach will be the same mindset that will get you bored shitless!'

And so I made my way back to Australia where I continued working for the previous company (remember, Australia's answer to Tony Robbins) and saw things morph into a company that valued its own profitability over doing the right thing by the client. Over and over again, I started seeing clients getting 'screwed' by the company, these clients who were now friends were starting to lose money hand over fist. The final straw for me was when they said – 'Goro, we want you only to sell this product and nothing else'. I knew deep in my heart that the product wasn't going to work and it would lose clients' money. I then chose to exit the company. Of course, I was right, somewhere between $7 Million to $30 million has been lost by that particular product with that company as of November 2016. I learnt a lesson, an important one –

'Your informed intuition is usually correct. As long as you listen to your intuition about doing the right thing, life will reward you.'

I was pissed. So pissed off that I left the money owing to me and started up a company. This company was going to be different. I was going to follow my own path and show people how to create true wealth the ethical way. This was how 10 properties in 10 years was born.

What we do at 10 properties in 10 years is provide authentic property mentoring showing our clients how to build their very own property empire – the same way I did. While I was setting up the business, I decided on five things –

a) We do this ethically

b) Keep it small and personable

c) We create massive wealth for ourselves and our clients doing this

d) We create RAVING FAN clients

e) I started this up as if I owned nothing

Now that last one is weird, I know, but let me share the small journey around that. I left Melbourne, my home town and went to Sydney, both to spend time with my fiancée (soon to be my wife) and also worked for a company and got mentored on how to do the first 3. I had decided to put myself in a difficult situation and worked as if I had no savings or previous wealth (apart from my wealth of knowledge). Why? I realised that in order to create true change in myself, I had to re-invent myself and if I used the monetary resources I had in the past, I would still have the older mindset. The lesson I learnt here was –

' In order to create a new you, you have to go through pain – your choice is for life to take you through it, or you create it yourself.'

I worked in Sydney for this property company for a year, in that time, I learnt what was ethical in the industry and what was unethical. By far the biggest lesson I learnt was around my true wealth and this put things into perspective. This was one of the toughest years of my life, as I learned to live once again on next to nothing, while having access to it all.

I went through huge emotional ups and downs, but always kept the end goal of re-creating myself in mind. It was only towards the end of this one year journey in Sydney, that I realised my issue around my wealth wasn't the resources, but was putting things into perspective and allowing myself to realise my true potential. My lesson was –

'Stop masking your true wealth – true wealth begins from within.'

After this experience for a year, I made my way back to Melbourne and decided to take over my parent's finance company (as Dad was approaching 65). Not only did I take this over, but gave it a complete overhaul rebranding it to a Yellow Brick Road franchise (Andrew Morello had been chasing me to do this for 5 years!).

Within a year of me taking over, not only did I use my previous skills to enhance the business but I grew it massively - where it just used to be Mum and Dad plus 1 employee in the business, I now have 6 employees working in the companies, each with their own cost centres and making a profit. The lesson learnt here was –

'Once you remove the block from owning yourself, wealth from money as well as wealth from the universe, money will flow into your life as if it was always supposed to be.'

Yes, working in these business's while planning a destination wedding with the love of my life is a challenging balancing act, but with money not being as much of a concern anymore, better quality conversations are to be had.

'Money won't solve all your problems, but it will allow you to get to the solution in a more efficient and effective way.'

I now have a share in over 23 properties and have 3 successful business's. What's more important to me is that I have both a family and a fiancée that I love. I don't say this to impress you, but rather to impress upon you that you have the same capability and time I do.

People ask me – Goro, how do you manage to fit so much in? I say the following to them -

'Time is the only thing equal to you and I, use yours to make yourself better, otherwise someone else will find a way to!'

Finally, I would love to give you the same gift I give to the people around me every day. I ask my staff members every day to start with their mission – their why. Here are mine -

Life mission –

To be a catalyst for massive financial change and to help create millions of dollars for the people I interact with every year!

Momentum Education Finance -

To help facilitate the everyday Aussie to attend life changing events right NOW!

10 properties in 10 years –

To provide Authentic Property Mentoring helping our clients build their very own property empire!

Yellow Brick Road Preston –

To help our clients achieve their hopes and dreams by providing them with the most awesome finance and mortgage advice we can!

Sure, there are always and always will be challenges in life. However, the point of this is that if this Indian – Aussie immigrant boy who started with nothing is here driving this McLaren – why can't you? I hope to meet you one day along our paths, should they choose to meet!

Live with passion and start with your why!

Chapter 6

Embracing Change

By Kiri Devi

This is a story of some pivotal moments in my life. Moments that changed the direction of my life, changed who I am …… forever.

We all have such moments.

"Joan is not working hard enough and we doubt she will attain the necessary result to pass her Matriculation exams."

These were the words I read in my school report card as a 16 year old in my final year of Secondary schooling in 1965. Twenty months earlier on my birthday, October 10th 1963, my father was operated on for breast cancer. My mother went to Adelaide, over 250 km's away, to be with him while he was in hospital. My 17 year old brother and I, at just 15, took over running the household and farm, together with my older brother, his wife and five young children under five, who lived on an adjoining farm.

We all thought Dad would have a reasonably short stay in hospital and then continue his recovery at home. Serious complications developed and 10 operations, several times being called to the hospital when my father was not expected to live, and almost two years later, my parents finally returned home. My dad had lost almost half his weight, had about 8 rib bones or part of them removed, had gaping, weeping holes in his chest that my mother dressed daily and could barely walk a few steps. I remember looking at him and thinking "that man is not my Dad. The Dad I knew has gone."

My marks at school had plummeted.

As I slowly read those words again I bit back tears of sadness and grief. Every one of my teachers knew my situation, yet only one out of about a dozen had ever asked me how I was coping or showed any concern for me; only concern for my grades, or my diary being signed by my parents and not my brother!!

As the sting of failure and shame of my failing grades washed over me, tears welled in my eyes. I had always been amongst the top quarter of students, now I was amongst the bottom and failing. My teachers didn't understand my situation.

As I re read my report card and allowed my feelings to flow something else washed over me. Anger. Rage. Rage at the insensitivity and lack of caring of my teachers. With this anger, this rage, a new thought, a new attitude, a change of mind happened. I made a decision, a new decision. I made a stand and backed myself. I was determined and committed to myself. I was going to pass no matter what it took. For almost three months I stayed up very late and got up at 4.00 am every morning. I learnt the entire Maths and Chemistry text book formulas and important facts off by heart. I didn't understand what I was learning just hoped I would at least apply the correct formula to a question. Now called Year 12, I passed Matriculation!!

I was accepted into Teachers' College and that is how I became a Junior Primary Teacher for 10 years, Deputy Principal Junior and Primary Schools for thirty more years and a few short times as Acting Principal.

A week after my exams I had forgotten the lot and had learnt that passing and grades were important, understanding was not, my feelings were not important, together with huge doubts and fears about my intellectual ability since I really didn't understand much of what I had written in the exams.

My life has been a quest for understanding ever since.

Now, many years later, I can look back and be grateful for those words of my class teacher. I realise the gift that he gave me in that experience of judgement and indifference to my pain and struggling. He called forth in me a strength, a determination and resilience that as life unfolded I would need many, many times. I have come to understand that all experiences and emotions are to be welcomed. Emotions are our teachers to our authentic being and must be acknowledged, felt, accepted, released and let go in order to grow and learn and embrace changes in our lives, to be responsible for our lives and not become a victim to life events.

"Rage is not innately ugly. That which summons it usually is."

~ Unknown

My father lived for over 11 years after his first operation and passed away in January 1975.

This was another pivotal moment in embracing change.

The year of 1974 had been particularly challenging: the builders of a new home my husband and I were building had gone into bankruptcy twice, making the building process very long and difficult. My sister in laws marriage had ended, she became ill and I cared for her three children for several months at the same time I was given a short Acting promotional position in my career. Then my mother came and stayed with me as my father was hospitalised for the final stages of secondary bone cancer.

I felt enormous sadness and grief at the loss of my father. I was the youngest of six children and our family (as many families were back in that era) had never been one to express emotions openly, never been parents that showed lots of affection and said I love you, never been parents who openly shared their thoughts and feelings and discussed issues with their children. I realised how little my education system and the generational socialization process of my family had really taught me about what I truly valued. My Dad was gone and there were so many things I wanted to share with him, know about him and for him to know about me. I wanted him to truly know how much I loved him and now it was too late.

In my grief I went searching. I read books, went to seminars on anything to do with personal development, health and well-being and started pouring all my emotions, thoughts and memories onto the pages of personal journals trying to understand this process of life and death. I had several deeply profound Spiritual experiences that back in 1975 I was too afraid to share for fear of being thought of as weird.

It was after my father's death that I wrote my first poems, or more accurately the poems were written through me.

Your Last Gift of Love on Dying.

(in memory of a man I loved dearly- my father)

Yesterdays can't be changed

Tomorrows may never be

Time is here, now, now, now

Every beautiful moment to be treasured

Yet even in death you gave

Will this sadness never leave me?

This overwhelming sadness of loss

But even this sadness is beautiful

Did it take your death to awaken feeling?

Did you ever know how much I loved you?

How much I missed of me- and you

~ August 1975

Those early experiences in finding my own strength, determination and resilience served me well during some of the challenging times in my life.

The year of 1990 was another challenging year of change.

Two of my sisters were diagnosed with cancer and both came to live with myself, my husband and three young children for several months before their final admission to hospital and their death. Amidst the loss and grief it sparked in me even more determination and desire to understand the mind body spirit connection to health and well-being and to understanding how our thoughts, feelings and attitude impact our lives.

I also came to understand the power of story and the power in the saying "we are only as sick as our secrets." It is part of my healing and my hope that in sharing my story this may also help others.

The Year of 1990. Too Young Too Soon

Too young, too soon

My two sisters

Lost to cancer

One 48, one 51

Your life cut short

exactly eight months apart

in that terrible year of pain and grief

My incredible mother

As she sat by your sides

Giving so much love, energy and time

Grieving inside

At 80

Asking the question

Why you my daughters?

Why not me?

Took with you your secrets

Of your woundedness

Your emotional pains, scars,

unresolved hurts, guilt, fears and blame

Only towards the end sharing

some of the burdens you had carried with you

The shame you felt that was too much to share

One sister buried on my eldest son's 10th birthday

My other sister buried on my youngest son's 4th birthday

A strange coincidence marking the celebration of both life and death

And a stark reminder to live life to the fullest

in the moments between

To love to the fullest in the moments between

My sister Olive a wonderful teacher

Almost 30 years of loving and giving to

children, their families and to her colleagues

Respected and loved so much they converted

the school shelter shed into a hall

And called it the memorial Hall in her name

Invited my mother to cut the ribbon

Officially open it, make a speech, draw the raffle

She pulled out my ticket

I won the raffle

I felt you were there

guiding her hand

A message to me somehow

I never knew your story until it was too late

Stories need to be shared

It is how we heal, in reaching out to others

It is in our vulnerability and in our sharing

we find strength

Together

My sister Beryl

You never did tell your story

Simply said "when your time is up, it's up"

My two sisters

Lost to cancer

One 48, one 51

Too young, too soon

~ Written may 2013

One of my mentors Anthony Robbins has a saying that your life is either a warning or an example. The death of my two sisters was a warning and further fuelled my desire to understand the connection between mind, body spirit, well–being and fulfilment. I embraced more books, seminars, journal writing and changes toward more physical self-care. Since that time a third sister and two brothers have survived cancer. My third sister after being in remission for over 10 years now has secondary cancer.

The year of 2009 brought huge change and challenges to grow some more.

In 2009 my life as I had known it fell apart. I had just retired from a successful forty year career in education, my husband ended our forty year marriage and our last two adult children had moved out of our home a few months earlier.

I lost my identity as a professional person, lost my identity as a wife, lost my identity as a hands-on mother, and lost my financial identity as someone with a secure ongoing income. I was 61, alone, in pain, grief, sadness, loss, anger, shock and bewilderment. I finally had to look closely at the questions "How did this happen to me" and did I want to become "bitter or better"?

I felt broken and lost and didn't know how I was going to mend myself.

My story is a story of my process of embracing the changes, of transforming my wounds. To paraphrase some of my teachers; it is aspirational not arrival, it is a journey not a destination, it is progress, not perfection. It is a continual work in progress, layer upon layer of healing and transforming old wounds into new insight, understanding, forgiveness and compassion and then applying this learning in my life. It is a continuing journey from my head to my heart.

Journey

The most courageous journey

Is the journey within

The longest journey

Is from the head to the heart

Just do it

You will be blessed

And those blessings

Will be sprinkled into eternity.

~ Written 2013

As part of my healing I sought counselling and was asked to write what may be the gift and learning amidst the pain. This was my answer from deep within.

I Have Come to Learn

I have come to learn that consciousness is the guiding force of all life.

Awareness is necessary to expand consciousness and open the door to love.

I have come to learn we are one,

that what I do, how I be, impacts all living things.

I have come to learn that I do make a difference,

and only I can decide what kind of difference I want to make.

I have come to learn that all events of my past

were necessary for me to gain the understanding and awareness I have now.

This will be the principle that guides me into my future.

I have come to learn

that our emotions are the key.

I have come to learn that all behaviour

is either a cry for love or an extension of love.

I have come to learn.

I have come to learn

to be in awe and gratitude of the creativity of the human mind.

I have come to learn

Love is the one power we can all share that increases all of life.

I have come to learn that everyone is doing the best they can

with the understanding and beliefs they have adopted as truth.

I have come to learn that the decisions I make today will impact my behaviour.

My behaviour will forge my character, my character will determine my destiny and my destiny will leave a legacy either life destroying or life affirming.

I have come to learn that accepting and expressing my emotions fully, frees me from the past so that I can live in the now and create a joyous future.

I have come to learn that behaviour is either a mask of fear

or a shining light of the vastness of our love, of our possibilities.

I have come to learn that forgiveness of others is the key

that unlocks the door to forgiving myself and is necessary to truly begin to love myself.

I have come to learn it is necessary to love oneself first

before I can truly love someone else.

I have come to learn that all events in life are simply an opportunity to heal, to choose to either shut down in fear or open in love.

I have come to learn.

I have come to love.

~ Sept 2010

I delved deeply into my feelings, accepted them, then let go in an exploration into loving myself more and claiming back my power and authentic being. An ongoing process.

> *"The wound is the place where the light enters you"*
>
> ~ Rumi

As It Is, Stay Open

Please be gentle with me at the moment

The wounds are very raw

I am hurting, I am angry

I am growing, I am learning

I will be stronger for it

I will be grateful for it

For these feelings are showing me

Where I am not valuing myself

Where I am not loving myself

The wound as Rumi says is where the light enters

Where the light of love penetrates the heart and soul

Bringing me home to my authentic being

Help me stay open to myself

To my heart, to my soul

Be gentle

The wounds are raw at the moment

As painful as it is

I also want to stay in this moment

Experience this moment

Feel this moment

Real, raw

As it is

So that I may be gentle with myself

Forgive myself, love myself

So that I may be gentle with others

Forgive others, love others

When they are hurting, angry

When they are raw, real

This is how compassion is born

Stay open, stay open

Feel, forgive, face truth

And unconditional love is illuminated

As I AM

After my marriage ended I plunged into learning by going to many different personal development seminars and courses and joining some online courses. This was how I met John Spender; at a course, never ever thinking I would become a friend of his, have the privilege of his wonderful, insightful coaching, or end up writing a chapter in his book! John is another one of those gifts of a person who is such an inspiration through his courage in overcoming adversity, his insightful coaching skills, compassion, spirituality and his belief in me in sharing my own unique voice and contribution in the world. My huge gratitude and appreciation to John.

I attended a series of seminars called Quantum Leap and at one, called Warrior Camp I did things that were way, way, out of my comfort zone and challenged me to think beyond my self-imposed boundaries- "if I could do that, what else is possible?" I often describe the Warrior experience to friends as a physical, mental, emotional, and spiritual enema!! For me it was exhausting, challenging and brilliantly wonderful. At the end I was called to stand with three others in the middle of a group of three hundred participants to be acknowledged as one of the oldest participants over sixty. I learnt a valuable lesson. Do not ever let your age, whether it be young or old, determine your life and stop you from following your dreams and passions.

I decided to be more conscious of my health and well-being. I started going on walks through the beautiful natural bushland in our local National Park. I went along to a wonderful Raw Food weekend and learnt how to make an amazing selection of tasty, yummy, nutritious raw foods and changed my eating to about 70% raw food. I drank much more water. I chose to have coffee, sugar and alcohol on rare occasions and have continued to limit these substances. I put on my favourite music CD's and danced and sang along wildly in the privacy of my own home. I didn't just make a vision board I made a whole vision floor across about seven metres of a downstairs room! I found pictures for every area of my life and placed them on that vision floor! Within a few months without actually trying I lost about 12 kilos and could fit into clothes I had when I was thirty! Bonus!! I looked and felt much more energised and people started saying I looked ten years younger. I joined Meetup groups (if you are not aware of Meetup they are groups that are free to join in an amazing number of interests. They are an absolutely wonderful way to meet new people, have fun and learn new things). I joined about ten different groups and walked, danced, sang, pub crawled, picnicked, wined, dined, learned new skills, meditated, laughed, partied, met some great interesting people and made wonderful new friends. I joined Match and went on the adventure of meeting new men. I didn't find romance with any but have remained friends with some.

I plunged into more learning about myself and how life works.

In 2010, standing at the luggage carousel in Sydney airport, about to attend another seminar I heard a deep voice say to me "Would you like me to collect your baggage for you?" Little did I know how significant this man, another John, would be in helping me get rid of my emotional baggage. I have such deep appreciation and gratitude for his friendship, support, presence, learning and growth in my life these past few years. John had recognised me from a face book photo of the seminar group and to our surprise we discovered we lived just seven streets away in the same suburb! As a birthday gift I invited him to a one day seminar on creating abundance where he met a woman who introduced him to the teachings of Shanti Mission. He invited me to come along to one of their meditation evenings. Again little did I know how significant this would be in shaping the direction of my life. Another set of coincidences! I will share about Shanti Mission a little later.

Meanwhile I continued to learn and grow.

Through a series of remarkable coincidences too long to share here, a friend introduced me to Trish. Trish was a Theta Healing practitioner. I booked a healing with her and it was powerful. I also took some of my poems and shared them with her. Trish immediately said "you have got to share these, they can help other people. I'll make it happen if you agree." It took me six months to agree. I was so nervous about the thought of sharing such personal information.

That was how I came to have my first ever three hour public poetry event telling my life journey through stories and poems called "Poems for the Soul." Trish believed in me when I couldn't and worked with me step by step to make it happen. At the end, the small group of friends who came along, stood, some with tears in their eyes, and gave me a standing ovation. I was profoundly moved by their acceptance of my sharing. Since then I have read my poems in local cafe's and poetry groups, and have shared them on a regular basis at a monthly 'Friendly Street Poets' Adelaide group. I have also had another three hour 'Poems for the Soul' public event and plan some more in the future.

Sometimes we just need someone to believe in us so strongly that we begin to believe in ourselves. That was the special gift Trish gave to me and I feel blessed that our paths crossed. I continued to learn from Trish completing a Theta Healing weekend training and a "Heart of Public Speaking" course, culminating in a public event sharing a speech that was both spontaneous and authentically from my heart. An amazing experience!

After the "Poems for the Soul" event this was what I wrote in a card thanking Trish.

Dear Trish

Thank you for believing in me; (as you told me in the way Michelangelo saw David in the block of stone) sometimes we need someone to see in us what we cannot see in ourselves and then for that someone to believe in us so strongly that we begin to believe in ourselves.

Thank you for being that sometime and someone.

You are a treasure.

With love

Namaste

xx

Marie was another gift in my life who I will be forever grateful for. I decided I needed to give back something from all my learning and volunteered to become part of the event crew at some of the seminars I had attended. Again with my battered and bruised self esteem and confidence, I timidly arrived at my first volunteer crew event, wondering if I would be able to learn some new skills and be of assistance. Marie was the amazing crew leader and a most wonderful role model of strength, courage, wisdom, intelligence, compassion and outright fun, fun, fun! With Marie's belief in me and encouragement to bring out the fun and wild side I had kept under wraps, I again, learnt some new skills, regained some confidence and in one event spent a lot of the time dancing at the front of the room encouraging the participants to get up and "Move It". Great fun and wonderful friendships made. My heartfelt love and appreciation to Marie and all the crew members for taking me for a "walk on the silly side" and helping me rediscover some disowned parts of myself.

One of the online courses I undertook was with Barbara Marx Hubbard and the Shift Network. As part of that course we were asked to meditate in silence for the first hour after waking each morning. Then we were to journal the answer to the question "Dearly beloved what do you have for me today?" with the Beloved meaning our Higher Self.

I was astounded by what flowed out of me!

Here is an example from the day 23 August 2012

Dearly Beloved what do you have for me today?

"I love beauty. Beauty in all its forms: in the colours of the rainbow, the flowers in all their wondrous shapes, colours and forms, the wind softly teasing the stalks of wheat or barley, or oats across a sun drenched field of golden crops, the majestic mountains, their blueness in the distance, a field of Salvation Jane displaying its full colour to the world, the smile of a baby, innocent and charming that opens your heart,

paintings, buildings, design and technology. I love creation, that's what I love, creation, inventiveness to create beauty in all its myriad of forms.

You must find your own beauty within, find that beauty that resonates within you. That is your particular gift or gifts to the world. Together we create a beautiful tapestry of life. Just as with all creation it can be jarring, distorted, even horrifying. The choice is yours, entirely up to you what you choose to create. And what you choose to create, in your life, WITH YOUR LIFE, affects the entire tapestry and is woven into the fabric of the entire tapestry of life. See, there is no small part to play because you are always a part of the bigger picture. So what part do you intend to play in the bigger picture? What do you envision for the bigger picture? Peace? then you must become that. Love? then you must become that. Light? then you must become that. You must become that which you are seeking. Embody those qualities and they will appear in the tapestry of your life and in the larger tapestry of all life.

About that shoulder thing, that tightening of the shoulders. It's a habitual thing. A waiting for life to give you a blow, a protective hunching. You can let it go, stand tall, be strong, be grounded. Let go of the cries of agony locked in your throat. Speak only of love and peace and compassion and understanding, of healing and wisdom. Speak only of the truth for that is who I AM, the truth. And the truth will set you free. Free to create whatever you want.

Let go of all your baggage and move lightly, joyously, divinely in this world. Shine your light on others. Be a guiding light. Be love. Be Peace. Be compassion. Be understanding. Be who I Am.

Your leg is about moving forward. Do not be afraid. Trust. Have faith. Let go of all the old baggage, the heavy load you are carrying around. Lighten up, find your beauty, find your beauty.

Words. Words have such great power in them. Choose your words carefully. They are creative, they carry with them their own energy. Words have power, great power. Use this power of words for love, for peace, for understanding, for compassion, for wisdom, for healing yourself and others.

Allow my words to come through you. You are never alone. I am with you always, all-ways. Trust, have Faith. Let go and let God. Let go and let God. Allow, let go of control, allow. Relax, relax your body and allow me to flow through you. Be a conduit of my love and light. Be a conduit for healing in this world. It is what you came to do through your Being. Let go and let God. Go about your day in love, peace and beauty. Be grateful for all the beauty that surrounds you, all the beauty that is within you. Create beauty wherever you go in all its many forms."

The Barbara Marx Hubbard on line course did two things for me. Convinced me that there was a greater power, whatever one may like to call it, that we could tap into. Secondly that at this moment in history we as a species needed to learn to live as a part OF Nature, not as apart from, and domination over nature, for our own survival. For the first time in our evolution we are at a point where we have the ability to consciously choose a pathway to probable destruction as a species or a pathway to possible peace and sustainability. That pathway begins within each one of us. If we each find peace within we may find peace without. We are all interconnected. All One. The consciousness of love and compassion is a choice and our way to evolve and thrive. First we must look deeply at ourselves, our thoughts, our feelings, our actions, take responsibility, and make a choice to change.

I was ready to delve deeper into the Shanti Mission School for the Soul and the teachings of its Founder, Sri Shakti Durga (formerly a Sydney Barrister).

When I first started going to meditations with Shanti Mission I was rather sceptical. Shanti Mission is a multi-faith school and uses chants and other practices based on the deepest truths from a range of religions, traditions and cultures, many from the Indian Hindu tradition. I realised I was making judgements about both Shakti Durga and some of the chanting/meditations. I decided to go to a week long retreat led by Shakti Durga to gain some more knowledge and understanding as opposed to judgement. There I met Shakti Durga, listened to her discourses and had a profound realisation that I was witnessing an ancient cultures mythology, symbolism and practices to understanding how life works. Similar to my experiences after the death of my father I had the profound experience of being connected to all of life. It was such a privilege and incredibly heart opening, and humbling to be in the company of fellow truth seekers, all wanting greater peace within themselves and Peace in the world. I soaked in the wisdom, compassion and love that Shakti Durga brought and I was forever changed.

Later I attended another week long retreat that was equally amazing, filled with reverence, awe, growing edges and deeper understanding, forgiveness, compassion and love for myself and others. It was at this retreat I was given a spiritual name Kiri Devi, the essence of which is to bring more light into my being and into the world, a continuing learning and growing into this name by releasing the blocks to love and light and connecting and embracing higher thought forms, emotions and actions.

This was a poem I wrote in the middle of the night at the second retreat.

Humbled

A kaleidoscope of the events of my life tumbled through my mind

Events of such synchronicity that it was impossible not to believe

There was a hand orchestrating them, directing my life, leaving me clues.

As I lay awake at four in the morning

Tears of awe and wonder

Streamed down my cheeks

I realised the incredible orchestration of events the Great Spirit, the Supreme Being, the Universe, the Quantum Soup, God, call it what you will had conspired to bring me home to me.

For a brief moment

In the darkness of the night

I got a glimpse

Of that profound love for me

I was humbled

I was Love.

~ June 2014

I am blessed to be part of a beautiful spiritual community of caring, supportive, learning, growing and fun-loving, people both here in my home town Adelaide and within the wider community of Shanti Mission. A gift of coincidence and synchronicity from a then unknown man called John who picked up my baggage in an airport. Blessings to you Ganga Dev, now his Spiritual name.

My marriage had been troubled for most of our 40 years together. My partner had struggled with an addiction for most of those 40 years and after the breakup I realised I also had a co- dependency addiction. As with many addictions there were episodes of domestic violence in its many forms. While I felt I had a successful professional career, in my personal life I felt very much a failure and much shame.

Addictions are painful and pain fuelled. It is painful for the person addicted and painful for the partner and family members. Often it comes with abuse in many shapes and forms and a slow, bewildering loss of clarity to see the situation for the truth. Power games of manipulation and control play out together with an insidious loss of self-esteem and self-worth. A deep sense of shame was at the core of my life. That is no longer there and is healed. I am stronger, wiser more understanding, forgiving and loving because of it and can now feel gratitude and appreciation for all my experiences.

During the last year of my marriage I also had the most challenging year ever in my teaching. I was sharing a class of what I experienced as the most behaviourally difficult and most academically and socially challenging class I had ever had in my forty year career. As my marriage imploded and I struggled with how to best help these children I found myself sobbing on the bathroom floor early one morning before work pleading, "Why? Why have you given all this to me?" To my surprise immediately an answer dropped into my mind. "When will you ever set some boundaries"?

The Mirror Glass Looking Deeply

You were just the mirror glass looking deeply
Reflecting back to me my own deepest beliefs
My deepest doubts about myself
My own worst fears of who I am
Of what I deserve
Revealing a reflection of me
My own loss of being
Loss of authenticity
Buried deep within my subconscious
Unknowingly playing out my life
Treated me so disrespectfully
So devalued me, then almost as if I didn't exist
The wounding so brutal, in that one action,
In that one lie, negated me, negated my being
Really it was just a re-opening
of wounding from a distant past,

my own disrespectful devaluing

and buried existence of myself

Now ready to heal

once I understand

That is how life works

with the gift of wisdom

To change wounds to wings

If only we dare to look and feel

through our pain

If only we can stay present to the hurt.

The anger, the betrayal of ourselves.

Not repress it back down again

and be closed off to the life within

Allow the searing burning through of emotions

to finally soar in understanding, forgiveness and love

Take full responsibility for attracting this to me

Correct the misperception

Understand with compassion, forgiveness and love,

the pain of that little girl long ago

Who gave up her authenticity

to be accepted by others

and rejected herself

Waiting for the courage to heal

and soar in freedom

from Wounds to Wings

There was always only Love.

~ October 2012

I now understand that often painful emotions are around setting boundaries for ourselves. To respect, accept, care, love and honour ourselves enough to set limits to behaviour. In doing so those expectations carry with them the belief that others have within them the power to choose different actions. They may not choose to. It is a free will zone. There simply will be consequences, and we must be prepared to live with the consequences of our choices.

On a grander scale I believe we are collectively at a point where we are being called to set some boundaries to our collective behaviour of destructive and abusive actions to our only home Mother Earth. We are being called to have faith and a belief that we can collectively choose to have more respectful, loving, caring attitudes and behaviour to all humanity and all living beings and live in harmony and sustainably on our exquisitely beautiful home. Called to live in Peace as one family.

Imperfectly perfect

And so we come to that Great Spirit

That is one within all of us

Imperfectly perfect

For the healing we must make

On our return home

To our authentic being.

~ October 2012

The above poem was to be a predictor of what my journey these past few years has been about – a journey into love, a journey into self-love, into loving others more openly and fully, A love that through forgiveness has both the gentleness and power to become kinder to oneself and others, a love that through understanding rather than judgement, embraces all as necessary learning on the path to discovering the true essence of ourselves which unites us all, a love that fuels creation, is fierce about protecting and setting boundaries and ultimately sets us free.

I know that this is just a beginning. There is much more to learn. There is much more for me to become and to take action in contributing toward a more loving, peaceful and sustainable world. I know I am a much more peaceful person, much more open and flowing with the opportunities that arise, and yes, at 68, there are exciting new beginnings and more changes to embrace.

I am currently studying with the Robbins Madanes Center for Strategic Intervention, and continuing studies with Shanti Mission, Authentic Education, and others online. I am so grateful for all the richness of experiences, relationships, mentors and learning in my life and now want to give back, share my experiences and learning and help others.

I have just recently registered my own Business "Understanding for Peace" I am developing ideas, finding resources and creating programs based on the 7 step process of my own journey of embracing change. This has been a journey through Understanding, Forgiveness, Love, Power, Joy, Fulfilment and Peace. I know I still have much to learn and grow into and that is what this adventure of life is all about!

One of my visions is to create a Forgiveness Garden as a symbolic way of burying past pain, hurt, sadness, anger, grief, shame guilt and remorse as we are planting plants that will grow and be transformed into something that brings beauty joy and peacefulness. Yes I love beauty!

I am deeply grateful and have such love and appreciation for all the people who have helped me walk this path on the journey of inner transformation and inner riches. The journey of embracing change and discovering the riches within continues.

Inside

Love softens

Love strengthens

Love creates

Look inside and set Love free

People of the world

~ August 1976

Love is Calling

Love is calling

Calling to you

Will you take up the challenge?

It's imperative that you do.

The challenge to love you

All of you.

The you that makes mistakes

The dark side, the angry, vengeful parts

Love the you that feels ashamed

of things you have done or not done

The things that you have put judgements on

and found unacceptable

Will you love you

fully, wonderfully, ecstatically?

So that you can love others.

It's imperative that you do

For all our survival

A moment in history has come.

Can you hear love calling?

The world needs you

and your love.

~ April 2011

In memory of my Mother and Father who gave me the gift of life. In Gratitude and Love

Joan/ Kiri Devi September 2016

My Heartfelt Thank You

Embrace Love.

Chapter 7

Change is the Only Way Forward

By Kelvin Kuan

Change is upon us.

In fact, the reality is that change is always upon us.

Change happens, change is happening, and change will happen.

Constancy is an illusion.

The reality (to most of our discomfort) is that change is the only constant in life.

It is our sensitivity that brings our attention to the change around us.

And on our life journey, it takes courage for us to change accordingly.

What we wear in summer, we don't wear in winter.

We change because it is time to change.

The signs of autumn are to prepare us for the coming winter, for the coming change.

And those who are in-tune will change accordingly.

Whilst those who aren't sensitive or are stubbornly passive

Will have to suffer the harshness of winter when it comes.

I have begun to see the critical importance of change as a personal choice, and as I prepared to write on this, I reflected long and hard about the concept of personal change because it is the single most important thing we can control in a world where we have no control. It comes as no surprise that Gandhi wisely recommended that we be the change that we want to see in the world. The external is constantly changing, regardless of us. Seasons change, people and events change, environments change. We can influence but not outright change the externals--- certainly not without considerable stress and misery. However, we can and must take responsibility for internal change. Doing so opens us up to new, previously unimagined worlds of opportunities and personal growth. Thus, it is worthwhile to practice the art and science of personal change.

By practicing personal change as a conscious choice, we can steadfastly face whatever is in our lives, whatever has happened, is happening, or will happen.

This develops an inner steadiness to face outer changes when they happen.

Personal change as *a choice* is something that can be practiced,

And it is best to cultivate this practice before external forces demand that we do so, so that we do not have to hit rock bottom or suffer tremendously before making changes.

So how do we *practice personal change*?

Reflecting on my own personal life and the lives of people that I know, as well as contemplating the stories of people that I deeply respect, I can distill the practice into a process of three parts: Recognizing Feedback, Confronting Fear, and Stepping in Faith.

I will spend the rest of this chapter to explain how mindfully going through this 3-part process of practicing personal change will develop inner confidence and outer success.

Recognize Feedback

To practice the art and science of conscious personal change, first we have to realize that there are clues and signs around us all the time, giving us feedback about the possible necessity for change. Awareness is a powerful sense to develop. Being aware, being sensitive to clues and cues around us---this is the first part to cultivate.

Recognizing feedback can be as small as being aware of those around you, to as big as noting the season of transition for a particular industry or country. Life is constantly providing feedback, on a micro as well as macro level. Some require immediate attention for change, whilst others require contemplation for subsequent changes. *By learning to recognize feedback, we are learning to see connections occurring in our lives so as to distinguish what are the appropriate changes we must make.*

Not too long ago, my life had reached a point where it was stagnating. It was not a sudden thing but rather, it felt like it had been building up to that point and I had just been insensitive to the signs up to that moment. Or perhaps I had been ignoring these signs or just hoping things would get better. But it was a long time coming, and clues were all along the way, and finally after a certain period, it became too hard not to notice. Not only were people and relationships in my life repeating in non-progressive patterns, but even my external environment showed obvious signs about change needing to happen.

I was working as a marketing consultant and private strategist when my projects started winding down all around the same time with nothing new on the horizon. Then one day, I noticed that the boutique hotel across the street from my office had closed. I was so wrapped up in my own world that I hadn't even noticed prior to that day. Within that same week, to my shock, I realized that my area was in the midst of change that I had not previously noticed. The small supermarket a few doors down from my office closed within that same week, and my favorite restaurant that I frequented just a block away decided not to renew their lease and was also gone within a few days. In fact, my office, which was shared with two different start-up companies, also moved out the month before. It could all have been a coincidence, and I could have chosen to dismiss it as such, but the convergence of all that happened within that period of time was too startling to ignore.

I spent several days contemplating the most recent events, as well as looking back further to events leading up to that present moment, and concluded that I had to make decisions for change. Recognizing the feedback from what was around me and in my personal life helped me come to the point where I could acknowledge this. The change I knew I had to make was actually quite major: I had to move. All around me was drying up, and closing down. The macro factors and micro factors provided sufficient feedback to me, and it was my choice to accept the feedback and make a change; or to do nothing and continue to put up with whatever harsh winter that may arrive after these warning signs of autumn had already begun showing up.

It may be difficult to recognize feedback in today's rush-paced modern life but it is there regardless, and it is absolutely important to take time out for oneself and be calmly reflective enough to pick up on it. How we feel is vital internal feedback about our current state of life. Learning to honestly ask ourselves about what we truly feel, no matter how messy our emotions may be, is a healthy exercise in learning to recognize this internal feedback mechanism we are born with. It is the exercise of going past our reactions to how we actually feel that helps us recognise the signs.

External feedback comes from our interactions with the world around us; often via people, patterns, and peculiarities. Your intuition is able to make connections from the external feedback if you relax and trust the grace within you. *Overall, the practice of recognizing feedback involves taking time out for yourself (each day, or in moments when they occur) to gently reflect upon areas of your life, feelings that arise within you, or external occurrences that stand out to you.*

Feedback is given for a simple reason: in the short-term, it is for contemplation and consideration; and then immediately thereafter, it is for action to be undertaken.

Consider the feedback we get when there is something potentially harmful or unhealthy that comes our way. It can manifest in our body, in our mind, our emotions, or in our surroundings. It is giving us feedback. Take for example, pain. This is a sign to get our attention, contemplation and consideration. If we ignore the root of our pain, it will return with increased intensity or in other complicated ways to our detriment. Accepting feedback, contemplating the issue of it, and its connection to us---will bring us into seeing things as they truly are, thereby prompting us to take action and make personal changes. Refusing to make changes when necessary will result in perpetuation of certain habitual patterns that eventually turn into huge problems. Thus, the most important thing we can do is to recognize feedback, and then consider and contemplate the action to take for personal change.

Some personal changes may be big, others may be smaller. Nonetheless, recognizing the clues, signs and cumulative feedback will confront us with the question: Do we choose to change or do we choose to do nothing. *It is important to note that passivity is also a choice, though more often it is an unconscious choice.* Even so, *the consequences of passivity are still ours to bear*, and at times its ill-effects do spill onto others as well. Thus, big or small, practicing a conscious choice for personal change is important.

For the past 33 years, I have looked in the mirror every morning and asked myself: 'If today were the last day of my life, would I want to do what I am about to do today?' And whenever the answer has been 'No' for too many days in a row, I know I need to change something.

~ Steve Jobs

Take a moment each day to ask yourself this same question that Steve Jobs asked himself.

Ask this for different areas of your life. Then come back to the pivotal question: what do I need to personally change?

Confront Fear

After we have learnt to recognize feedback and considered the necessary action-steps for personal change, then we must confront fear. Confronting fear is crucial because the habitual pattern in human behavior when faced with difficulty is an inclination towards avoidance, convenience and comfort. Without dealing with fear, we are stuck in habitual patterns that do not promote growth but instead, cyclically reruns and a return to old and familiar ways.

It is amazing the amount of tolerance for pain that people will put up with, just to avoid changing. It is common for most of us to be stuck, frustrated, and complaining while continuing with the same self-sabotaging cycles and habitual patterns. Deep down, it's the fear of change that prevents us from confronting and moving forward. The old saying "Better the devil you know than the devil you don't" highlights this problematic human tendency towards resistance to change. However, it is important to realize that refusing to change when it is necessary will only prolong avoidance and nothing good happens when we do not do what needs to be done. Avoidance does not make issues better; rather it compounds the issues and makes them worse.

When the feedback around me caused me to reflect and realize that it was time for change, and that meant the possibility of a move for me, I was uncomfortable of course. I spent a few days letting myself take it in and just ponder what it would be like to take action for that change. Change hardly comes as a solitary event, but rather a collective of intertwining factors as well. Thus, it takes courage to face all this and yet commit to the action(s) that must be undertaken. I would be pretending if I didn't admit that there were fears and concerns. In my case, if I made a move, what did I have to do beforehand? Who did I have to inform? What do I say to them? Am I certain of myself? I would have drowned in the details had I not brought my attention back to the feedback that I had recognized up to that point. I learnt an important lesson during that experience: *change begins with an acceptance of the need for it and it is propelled by the decision to do so.*

Getting caught up in the details is often our fear mechanism operating in overdrive. There are certainly worthwhile concerns when undertaking any change, but there are also triggers from internal fears that arise anytime we move out of our comfort zone. Deciding involves committing a yes to one and a no to another; otherwise we unrealistically think we can have one without letting go of another, or we end up being burdened with two. This is, ultimately, not deciding. It is mentally hedging and trying to accommodate two options rather than actually choosing one. It happens only in the mind since it is impossible in real life to eat your cake and have it beautifully untouched. So, unless one chooses to let go of one and take hold of another, no decision has actually been made. And when time comes for a decision to be made, make it---rather than leaving options open on the table, past the time to actually make a decision. This will be akin to leaving fruits on the table past the time in which to eat them and now these fruits have started to rot.

Our inner strength is developed as we make decisions when it's time to do so. Deciding is simply saying yes to one and no to another, without leaving open options to rot on the table past a valid decision time. A binary (yes/no) framework, though limiting, actually helps sharpen our decisive effectiveness within the realistic boundaries of time. It is worth practicing so that we distinguish which scenarios truly require more thought before we make a decision, and which scenarios are simply our fears pushing us to indulge them instead of making a choice forward. The nature of time (passing away) demands that we make decisions; otherwise, it might be too late.

"So many people live within unhappy circumstances and yet will not take the initiative to change their situation because they are conditioned to a life of security, conformity, and conservation, all of which may appear to give one peace of mind, but in reality, nothing is more damaging...."

~ Christopher McCandless

The courage that comes from confronting fear in our lives is the single most powerful thing that happens when we choose personal change. It could be starting something new, heading in a new direction; closing a chapter of your life story. Change is always accompanied by newness, since change signifies a difference from the previous way. This is a good thing, because if the previous had been sufficient, there would not have been feedback and signs that change was necessary. Thus, something different is required, a change is needed. Accepting this and facing it with courage makes all the difference.

How do you dig deep into courage within you? Remind yourself that you recognize the feedback and signs for a reason. If you were unable to change, you would not have recognized those signs and feedback to begin with. It is a subconscious part of you that has become conscious of the change that you need to undertake. *Remember that choosing to stay in old patterns while expecting new growth possibilities is a form of fear-imprisoned madness. Remind yourself that fear only keeps you trapped, while making choices for change open you up to growth and new possibilities.*

The following few quotes below can help you develop courage.

Gently reflect on areas in your life that you know require change,

Make a note of the recognizable feedback and signs prompting for change.

Then as you read these quotes, feel which ones resonate with you.

Highlight the ones that resonate with you and let them deepen inside you.

"If we don't change, we don't grow. If we don't grow, we aren't really living".

~ Gail Sheehy

"Failure is not fatal, but failure to change might be".

~ John Wooden

"If you do not change direction, you may end up where you are heading".

~ Lao Tzu

"Change before you have to".

~ Jack Welch

"All changes, even the most longed for, have their melancholy; for what we leave behind us is a part of ourselves; we must die to one life before we can enter another".

~ Anatole France

"I cannot say whether things will get better if we change; what I can say is they must change if they are to get better".

~ Georg C. Lichtenberg

"We all have big changes in our lives that are more or less a second chance".

~ Harrison Ford

Take the time to let these nuggets of wisdom dissolve your resistance to change, especially when it is time to change. Find the courage in these truths from those who have lived successfully. Then you can move into the third part of practicing personal change.

Step in Faith

After recognizing feedback for change, and accepting the need for it by confronting our fear of it, then we follow through on our decision by stepping out in faith. This actually has a positive effect on us over time when we continually practice personal change because we reinforce our inner sense of capability when we move through change. This fact alone should give us tremendous encouragement. Fear of change is often a deeper fear of inadequacy on our part to deal with the unknown: What will happen? Can I manage? What will I do? All these questions stem from a fear of being out of control, and also the illusion that we can control the external so as to prevent any suffering. In truth, *the best we can do is develop our capacity for change and our capability during change.*

When I decided to make the move, I had only a few things that were confirmed. I had my flight booked, my first week of accommodation, and a portion of my savings with me. *The other thing I had which was probably the most important thing I brought along was my choice to be open.*

My scheduled flight was three days before the new year. I was not familiar with the place that I was going, except that it felt like the necessary step forward. I ended up experiencing one of the best new year experiences ever. Instead of being stuck in an overcrowded cluster of people clamouring just to watch a countdown with typical over-the-top fireworks in some huge city, I found myself within the historic moat of a small and charming Southeast Asian city where well-wishers were lighting up sky lanterns and offering their prayers and intentions for the year ahead.

There were crowds that were spread out and around but not packed like an unbearable concentrated swarm. For the entire night, sky lanterns went up continually, dotting the night sky like floating candles. The experience felt participative and communal because one could light their own sky lantern to join the thousands that had been lit and released up by others. It was a shared experience, a joint interaction and a collective celebration.

It was at that moment I understood why I made the change and what I was looking for. Even though I didn't have all the answers to the change I had undertaken, the reason became clear after I took the step of faith towards change and ended up experiencing this collectively-contributed participation. And within a month, I developed new capabilities as a result of adapting to this change that I had undertaken.

Taking that step of faith is the only way to close the circuit to personal change. *If we recognize feedback and accept the need to change, and do indeed confront our fears, then the necessary last part is to step by faith into whatever action that needs to be undertaken.* Otherwise, nothing happens—we've merely played a mind game with ourselves.

After I recognized the feedback that I ought to move, if I confronted my fears and yet did not purchase a ticket and taken the step of faith to go, I would not have had that new experience that sparked the deeper understanding of why I had to move. Most of us (me included) want to know the "why" before we take the next step. However, where change is concerned, once our intuition recognizes the feedback that calls for our change, then confronting fear and stepping in faith will eventually give clarity to the "why".

Stepping in faith means *taking action that the change requires.*

And there can be no overstating the importance of taking action as a step of faith. Without action, change does not occur.

"Action is a great restorer and builder of confidence. Inaction is not only the result, but the cause, of fear. Perhaps the action you take will be successful; perhaps different action or adjustments will have to follow. But any action is better than no action at all".

~ Norman Vincent Peale

"Inaction breeds doubt and fear. Action breeds confidence and courage. If you want to conquer fear, do not sit home and think about it. Go out and get busy".

~ Dale Carnegie

"Thinking will not overcome fear but action will".

~ W. Clement Stone

"Without change there is no innovation, creativity, or incentive for improvement. Those who [take action to] initiate change will have a better opportunity to manage the change that is inevitable".

~ William Pollard

"You see, in life, lots of people know what to do, but few people actually do what they know. Knowing is not enough! You must take action".

~ Tony Robbins

Taking action as a step of faith will eventually develop new capabilities in you, and *this leads to an inner confidence towards life because you experience your own growth and capability to adapt, navigate and thrive through changes.* The inner strength that comes from stretching and knowing your own capability is itself a life-transforming experience that affirms the personal changes you have undertaken. *So the truth is, even though we do not like change, it is the only thing that has brought about progress in our lives.*

And now you have it.

If you read all the way to here, you now have the process of personal change---clearly presented to you. It is now time to practice, and to experience it personally.

It is time to take action.

So look through the areas of your life.

Reflect and write down your responses to each of these parts regarding change.

Recognize Feedback: Are there signs for change?

Confront Fear: What fears do I need to confront?

Step In Faith: What actions do I need to take?

Take the opportunity to also reread the quotes and phrases in italics that stood out to you; let them sink deep in your subconscious mind as encouragement and motivation towards taking action.

Feel free to connect with me at writekelvin@gmail.com and share how this chapter has affected your life. I would love to hear from you.

"Change is difficult, and yet change is the only way forward".

Chapter 8

Never Give Up

By Teresa Elliott

Who am I?

I lay there alone for six weeks, the first six weeks of my life, a newborn. No one to bond with, just left there to wait for someone to love me. Unbeknown to me the universe was presenting me my first two lessons. Lessons would last decades into my life. The lessons were Abandonment and Trust.

I don't remember the first six weeks of my life being alone, but I know that I have never been afraid of being alone. Being adopted can throw so many elements of thoughts into your mind of not being worthy? And so many Why's, that you start to think, is it a word?

I am grateful my parents told me from a very young age that I was adopted, because I think if they had hidden the fact, it would have massively affected my trust issues to the point of no return.

I was chosen by my mother who is my rock! She has loved me unconditionally which I am truly grateful for. Thanks mum. I love you!

Mum said she chose me, because I was in the corner of a triangle room on my own, the eldest baby. I was dirty with milk stains and looked like no one loved me. She instantly chose me and in her mind was saying I am going to get her, clean her up and put her in a beautiful outfit.

My first five years were spent growing up in Griffith, a country town in NSW, Australia. I was surrounded by a big Italian family with lots of cousins. After five years we headed for a sea change to the Central Coast. I found out years later our sea change was to pick up my biological brother from hospital on the way. Just as we were leaving my parents got the call and suddenly, we were not picking up my brother. A brother I would never grow up with, play with, fight with or create a lifelong bond with.

My childhood was filled with lots of friends from school, surf lifesaving and the swimming club. My parents threw me into sport, which I embraced. Now knowing that it was a perfect foundation for me to feel strong within myself, for what I was to experience on my journey ahead. I was entering my teens and my life was about to do a flip, from strong foundations and friendships to solace.

In my early teens I was sexually abused whilst on school holidays. I won't go into details...It is what it is. This ate at me from the inside out, I couldn't hold this pain in any longer and a few years later, I was watching Oprah with my mum and Opera was talking about being abused and next thing you know, I was balling my eyes out. I couldn't contain it anymore, I had to express my emotions and feelings and the flood gates opened, what a release of pain, pain that I didn't have to hold in anymore, I could have my mum help me take that burden away and help me heal. When you hold feelings and thoughts on the inside, you feel so alone and ask so many questions of yourself, like will anyone believe me? Did I create this? How many other people has this happened too? Why would they do this to me? What makes them think this is ok? Who can I trust?

After coming out and telling mum, it spiralled to my whole family and friends knowing. The majority didn't believe me and were putting it down to me being rebellious and causing trouble and that I was on drugs. Which I wasn't, however that was the path I was about to take, I felt lost and alone. With people not believing me, I started to hang around the wrong crowd, take risks and I started experimenting with drugs – marijuana and alcohol. I would binge drink at parties and even drink before sport at school sometimes. All these issues raised my identity crisis, which I never even knew I had. Being Aboriginal puts you on the other end of the stick, you feel unworthy as society doesn't accept you. Was I Aboriginal, Italian and god knows what else? So I questioned being adopted, why was I given away, was it because I was unworthy of love?

Everything felt like the world was against me and I was nothing. One afternoon I sat in my room behind my bedroom door. I had next to me all my parents pills out of their medicine cupboard and a bottle of scotch, then I sat there in my room, swallowing pill after pill with scotch, after a while I was feeling quite floaty. I had a razor sitting there ready to cut myself to feel pain, I wanted to feel it, as the pain from the inside was overwhelming me. So with feeling floaty, I started to cut my wrists. I couldn't remember which way was the right way to cut them, so I cut them sideways and up my arm and kept doing this until I could see enough blood oozing out of me. Then I passed out.

Feeling pain didn't help, it only highlighted my demons. So I took the path of drugs and alcohol and partied, I became the life of the party and was up for anything that was fun and exciting. I continued this path for several years. This felt great! It gave me what I wanted – to feel numb! To feel nothing and not to think of the past and the pain that came with it. I now look back at those years and thank god I am still alive.

I lay in a corner of a room again. This time I was 24 and had just woken up from being a victim of Domestic Violence, and I had been out cold for quite some time. I woke up to see these big blue eyes staring at me in shock; it was my boyfriend's friend.

She asks me if I was alright and all I could say was "What the hell am I doing?" Why am I letting him have this power over me! I wouldn't normally let anyone have this power over me, but I was vulnerable and I was on a lot of drugs.

Things were about to change, I could feel it coming. I knew I was at rock bottom and I couldn't cope any longer, I couldn't suffer any more pain. It was like a storm of change was coming my way and I was going to ride that storm like a wave and embrace it. I know now that I need extreme situations to make changes. We all have different tolerance levels of what we will accept in our lives, until we hit that wall or go deep enough into that hole. That is when you ask questions of yourself asking why am I putting up with this, why am I accepting this? This is when your 'aha' moments can come.

You are worthy

My 'aha' moment was when I was sitting on a beach in Bali – the famous Kuta Beach. Six months after working and focusing on my issues, I decided to reward myself for leaving that relationship and everything that came with it, with a holiday for 'me'. I had just arrived with only a backpack and no accommodation booked, as I wanted it to be an adventure. So I made reservations at a resort in Legion, the neighbouring suburb from Kuta. Twenty minutes later I was at my resort and headed straight for the beach. I sat there in silence just watching the waves and looking around soaking it all in. I said to myself, "I deserve this! I survived and I am rewarding myself" - with a smile that I had actually achieved it. This would be the moment that would change my life forever. This holiday made me self-evaluate everything in my life. It made me realise I have the power to do anything and have control of it. Everything about this holiday changed my mindset to focus on me and only me.

I spent two weeks in Bali. It was the best thing I have ever done and it really changed my life. I spent most of my time alone, soul searching, asking questions of myself and really discovering what I wanted out of life. Also seeing how people struggle daily in other countries made it easier for me to be grateful for what I did have in life. Even though there was a lot of crap.

Don't ever forget to keep rewarding yourself, life is so busy and hectic these days, we forget to celebrate the little things. Once we start celebrating the little things in our life, the universe will present us with more of those amazing moments in life to celebrate. And we have all heard the saying before – "Your thoughts become things." Our inner voice can talk us out of things and feed our fear. Be in the now and focus on where you're heading, not what has already happened. I have had a bit of training in trauma management and they have proven that every time you re-live that horrific moment in your life, your mind, body and soul will relive it, like it is happening to you right now. Don't give that person or that thing the power over you! Know that you have survived it and it's certainly made you stronger. I know now that I can talk about my painful experiences without getting upset and that's because I own it, accept it and acknowledge that I have survived and it has made me stronger. Our mind is an amazing and fascinating organ.

It has incredible power to change our emotions and feelings can control our lives and how we live it. Don't focus on what has happened; focus on what you want to happen from now on. The world was created with an opposite to everything. For example, big and small, tall and short, hot and cold, good and bad and of course positive and negative. Which leads me to the game I play within my own mind. Everything has the opposite, so when bad things happen, there is always a positive to it. For example, being abused and being in a domestic violent relationship. I focus on surviving it, as I am now on the right path for my purpose in life, to help and support people who have suffered and I can relate where they are coming from. It can be hard to think like that, but there is always an opposite and it may only come to you years later.

A great way to practise this is to be grateful for what you do have. When you travel to many countries and see how other people live and what they accept, which is much less than you, it's easy to understand how to be grateful. Start your day with gratitude, acknowledging the things you DO have in your life. I do a journal as well as saying affirmations. I do this every morning driving to work. And everybody has something to be grateful for. Be grateful for your family, be grateful for being alive, be grateful for having a roof over your head, be grateful for your mind, be grateful for friendships and be grateful you are healthy. It is easy once you get started and practice it. Just watch the news and you will have a lot to be grateful for, as someone always has it worse than you.

Miracles do happen through gratitude!

Feeling bored and uninspired in my job, I was working in Government housing, I had to create things to do. I had just started being grateful each morning on my way to work, which made me feel good each day. I began to have overwhelming feelings to search for my brother. I applied for my original birth certificate through Family and Community Services. Last time I tried it was so hard to apply for I gave up, this time it was easy, I only had to provide my 100 points of identification. I sent it off and got excited, as it would only take six weeks to be delivered.

I'll never forget the afternoon my husband handed me the mail, I was on the phone to a previous employer who was offering me a job and my husband handed me the large envelope, I was wondering what's this? I had totally forgotten about my application, until I opened it. It actually took about twelve weeks to get to me, as they were busy over the Christmas break. I opened it and I became super excited, hung up the phone and went inside to start searching on the internet. I actually had a name to search for now! I searched and Genealogy came up, and there were five names, my biological mother being one of them. I typed in each name and had one to go. I typed this name in and I got something, a Facebook page. I couldn't believe my eyes, there was a young man who lived in Long Jetty, the same suburb as me! Is this real? It stated that he was my uncle in Genealogy, but I knew I had a brother five years younger and I went through his page and realised he was the age of my brother and the resemblance was freaky, I knew it there and then. I said to my husband "This is my brother!" whilst shaking and not knowing what to do with myself. I couldn't believe it. My husband was trying to calm me down, saying "Don't get to excited, it might not be, it was too easy, no one finds their family that quick." I replied, "Well I just did", convinced it was him. So I sent him a private message and waited and waited. I hardly slept that night. I just wanted him to reply.

Then mid morning the following day, I got a message back and this was our conversation word for word.

Teresa   21/3/14 @ 7.10pm

Hi Richard, This is a bit random, but are your parents Anthony and Irene Ruhl? I am trying to track down Lesley Anne Ruhl, is she your sister? Thanks and I hope your Friday has been good to you :) Cheers Teresa

Richard   22/3/14 @ 9.53am

Hey how are you Teresa? I've been flat out working. That was a random question hahaha. tell me about yourself are you a relative?

Teresa   22/3/14 @ 12.33pm

Hey Richard :) I can imagine, real estate business never ends, lol. Well, that's an interesting question too. Well I was adopted in 1976, and I just received my original birth certificate and it states that my biological mothers name is Lesley Anne Ruhl. I am not really sure if I am going to go down the track of meeting or disclosing who I am, as she may not want to or have told anyone either.

So for me it's just doing a bit of research and then I came across your name and funny thing is, is that I have grown up on the Central Coast and live in Long Jetty/Shelly Beach.

It totally spun me out, when I saw you had a business in Long Jetty, however we may not be related, but I thought I would just put it out there and see what happens.

I am aware that I have a brother whom is five years younger than me, however she decided to keep him, as my parents were going to adopt him also, however things changed at the time. So you're my first real lead from all this... :) Anyway, I hope I haven't freaked you out :) Have an awesome weekend! Hope to talk soon. Cheers Teresa :)

Richard   22/3/14 @ 1.51pm

I'm blown away.

Teresa   22/3/14 @ 1.52pm

So am I!!! I hope I haven't upset you or anything, don't even know if I am on the right path???? What are you thinking? T

Richard   22/3/14 @ 1.56pm

You are on the right path I just can't believe it. You have lived that close to me. I'm your brother; I can't believe it, are you ok?

Teresa   22/3/14 @ 2pm

Omg!!!! Are you sure you know? I think so, got a few tears, happy tears!!!I can't believe we have been so close either!!! I've lived here for 35 years!!!! Did you know I existed? X

Teresa   22/3/14 @ 2.05pm

I really hope I haven't upset you. Just after having kids, I have really wanted to find you, as I have known about you my whole life!

This is soooo freaky! I have butterflies!!!

***

Miracles do happen and dreams do come true! This experience really made me believe that practicing 'Gratitude' daily can really change your life. Just try it and see how things can magically change. I must admit I felt funny doing it at first, but then it came naturally. Just like this book opportunity. It just fell in my lap. Having it on my vision board is what spooks you, as I only put it on their six months ago and now here I am writing this chapter.

In all this greatness and happiness in my life, I looked back at what I was doing just before this all happened and I realised I helped it all happen. HOW, you ask??? Three months before this I was writing in my Gratitude journal daily, or as often as I remembered. I would say a mantra on my way to work every morning and this was all the things I was grateful for in my life. Prior to this I would ask the group in the program I facilitated the question "Who would you have dinner with, living or dead? I answered that question with the same answer for four years –"My Brother"!!!! . I know that saying these words and writing them down was a major role in it all coming together and being generally happy throughout it made the magic happen. We were even on a morning show, telling the country our story.

It hasn't been all roses since I found my brother. There have been some moments in my life recently where I have felt lost, due to reconnecting with my biological family. I have felt disconnected with my biological family; feeling left out and lost, due to not growing up with them and having the bonds that everyone had. I missed out on so much. Also feeling disconnected with the family that I did grow up with. But what I do know is that the more I talk honestly and openly about my emotions, things will heal and I won't feel lost.

Another thing I know for sure is having my brother in my life now, is one of the most amazing things I have done in life, besides having my three beautiful kids. We have a bond stronger than I think we could have had if we had grown up with each other, we know we will always be there for each other. I know I can trust him and believe in him, and he has been part of my healing for the lessons that were given to me in the beginning, that of abandonment and trust. I know we will never abandon each other and I know I can trust him, which is giving me the faith to not have those issues from now on. So the lessons my biological mother had given me of abandonment and trust, it is my brother that is healing them now. Even though we have grown up with different families and were raised differently, we are still so very similar in so many ways. I am only focusing on the great things we are yet to experience and achieve from here on.

I could focus on the whys and what if's, but it is what it is and I cannot turn back time. And if I could, would I want to? No, I wouldn't be here where I am today.

Making your mind change focus on different experiences can have a massive effect on your future. For example: I know all of my sufferings throughout life are or were really to help my future, as I now work as a Caseworker and I am completing my Diploma in Counselling. I help people in Mental Health and families that struggle from relationship breakdowns. I know I do my job well, as I am passionate about it and can relate to some things they may have endured personally. I get confirmation on this when I see previous clients and they can't help but tell me how their life has changed and they are doing well and thank me for helping them change.

It wasn't me that changed them. It was their own self, they decided to change their situation. I listened with no judgements and asked the hard questions. These moments are why I love doing what I do and it makes you feel alive, when you are a part of positive changes for people. We all have a story that is unique to us. I want to give you insight into my mindset and the elements of how I have overcome trauma and bad choices throughout my life.I truly believe that when you accept things, moments and people for what they are and talk about it honestly and openly, you can heal. You release the thoughts and the energy. Keep it locked up and that is what can make you sick.

Own who you are, embrace YOU!

Own your shit! No one is perfect and what IS perfect? We all have secrets and insecurities. I am no stunner, yet I own who I am, and this is what gives me confidence. I embrace all the good, the bad and the ugly. An exercise to help identify these things is to make a list of all the character traits you love about yourself and a list of traits you don't. These are your strengths and weaknesses. Take half an hour to really access what you love about yourself and what you don't love about yourself. Then start making goals and say positive affirmations to make those things about you more loveable. Things WILL change! Owning who you are will give you confidence. And confidence creates opportunities.

Know what your values are

Values are a way of knowing what makes you tick and what motivates you. Some we do naturally without even acknowledging them. These are the things that piss you off and what you're passionate about. And we can all name a few of them.

My top three values at 40 are: 1 – Family, 2 – Honesty, and 3 – Quality Relationships. Values can change over time, I know in my twenties, my top three values were, 1 – Socialising, 2 – Money and 3 – Work to make money to socialise.

Go to my website stand-up.com.au to do an exercise to identify your values and many other self-help tools to love yourself.

Focus and Goals

It's what you do next that counts! If you lie around and do nothing, nothing is going to change. So what you need to ask yourself when you're not where you want to be. Ask, "Where do I want to be?" (Sit in silence and ask) Your gut will tell you. Then ask and write down all the things you can do, actions that you can take to make small changes.

When we see stairs, do we expect to step right up to the top step; we know we have to take the little steps to get there, just like our goals.

Who cares what people think!

I don't know how I got this strength and skill naturally. As long as I can remember I have never really cared what other people think.

A quote I love.

> *"There is a huge amount of freedom that comes to you when you take nothing personally."*

We all have reasons why we do certain things. Why explain to people? They are not walking in your shoes on a daily basis, dealing with your problems and issues; they are not thinking the things that go through your mind? Don't give them the power to doubt yourself. Only you give them that power. Funny thing is, we can be focused on what others think, but everyone is walking around thinking the same thing. What will they think? So if we are all thinking that, we are not really paying much attention to others anyway. It's our mind focusing on it and giving it more power.

Creative Outlet

Having a creative outlet, releases pain, trauma and calms your mind, body and soul, just by doing something that gives you pleasure. For me it is cooking, reading, Reiki, meditation, crystals, arts n crafts and painting. This is what puts you in the state with your mind, body and soul to receive things from the universe. So when doing your creativeness, think, plan and dream of all the things you want in your life.

A great way to start, if you're lost, is to create a Vision Board. All you need is a piece of cardboard, magazines, photos and scissors, glue and some texta's and you just start pasting all things that you want in your life. It could be money, a new job, a holiday or two, your dream home, your dream car, health and happiness. The list is never ending. You then stick it up somewhere so you can look at it on a daily basis! This is what can help you focus on what you're striving for! Especially when you get caught up on a negative path.

My favourite quote is by a man I admire immensely – Tony Robbins.

"Where focus goes, Energy flows"

It is so powerful!!! Think about it, if we focus on something negative, so many elements come into place and we can create this massive story that isn't even true or factual. It's about acknowledging the negative and putting energy into positive things you want and next thing you know your motivated to take action.

A Positive Attitude – Being Optimistic

In every bad situation or scenario there is good. The world was created with everything having an opposite. The hard lessons are there to teach us. Every decision we make leads us to our situation. So look on the bright side of things. I know all my events are there to help me to do what I am passionate about, helping people overcome their pain and accept what has happened and make choices to start their future.

Good – Bad   Long – Short

Hot – Cold   Big – Small

Young – Old   High – Low

Positive – Negative

Everything has an opposite!

Meditation

People overlook how powerful this can be if you practice it often. I did this as a child without knowing, only realising in my late thirties that I was doing it and made me realise that was one of the key factors that helped me through my turmoil.

You can meditate anywhere in any position! As a child I used to sit in front of my dressing room table staring into the mirror and then going into a trance, and before I knew it, I was there for hours. I couldn't remember what was going through my head, as I was meditating. These days I have to go somewhere to meditate, due to my wonderful brain continuously thinking all of the time, especially at night. I am always thinking of a business idea or an invention, it drives me crazy!!! But when I meditate, I can fall asleep effortlessly and I am revived and pumped the next day, all fresh.

My Reiki teacher and meditation master has a beautiful mediation process, by taking you on a journey through colour first. This opens your chakras and then she takes you to a spiritual garden to then return down the colourful stairs to close your chakras. I do this on my three kids, who are all under nine and resist everything within themselves to sleep, and I have them asleep within minutes of this meditation story.

If you have never meditated, just try it a few times and you will be amazed at how grounded you become and your mind clears to focus on the important stuff in your life.

Connect to Mother Earth

Life is so busy these days and we are surrounded by technology, concrete and buildings etc. We need to connect to mother earth. This has an amazing affect grounding us. Hug a tree, walk barefoot on the grass, dirt or sand, feel the nature. Everything is energy and the more we love our earth the more it will love us.

This works wonders on children who may have high or special needs, as it connects them, grounds them and calms them. If you suffer from anxiety, go hug a tree, seriously, thank it for giving you oxygen and life. It will feel silly at first, but I can assure you, you will walk away feeling very different.

***

I truly believe that saying that 'Everything happens for a reason'. Don't try and analyse it or understand it, just believe and trust it. Throughout life we will be students and teachers, learning and teaching the lessons of life. Just know that we are forever learning and teaching all around us. The day we stop learning, we stop living. So embrace what life has to offer and embrace it all, just remember;

"Where focus goes, Energy flows"

I will end this chapter with a beautiful Native American Legend Poem.

Two Wolves

A Cherokee Legend

An old Cherokee is teaching his grandson about life. "A fight is going on inside me," he said to the boy.

"It is a terrible fight and it is between two wolves.

"One is evil – he is anger, envy, sorrow, regret, greed, arrogance, self-pity, guilt, resentment, inferiority, lies, false pride, superiority, and ego," he continued.

"The other is good – he is joy, peace, love, hope, serenity, humility, kindness, benevolence, empathy, generosity, truth, compassion, and faith. The same fight is going on inside you – and inside every other person, too."

The grandson thought about it for a minute and then asked his grandfather, "Which wolf will win?"

The old Cherokee simply replied,

"The one you feed."

Chapter 9

The Art of Becoming Resilient

My story, from my heart.

By Katrina Gulabovski

As I walked into the doctor's office with my mum and dad behind me, I was leaving the life I had known. The doctor had delivered a life-altering diagnosis to my dad that affected us all .. my mum, my three children, and I. Dad's test results determined he had dementia. I couldn't believe what my ears had just heard. I was in shock and numbed to the core as we left the doctor's office, walking into a life of uncertainty. The journey from level ten to the ground floor lobby was an excruciatingly slow one. It was in that moment that my life began to derail.

I had no idea how all of our lives would be impacted from that day forward. My emotions began to surge, followed by my mind flooding with so many questions, the answers to which were yet to be discovered along my journey. I started to question why? Why my dad? How did this happen? I was the one now caring for my children and my non-English speaking parents in their elderly years alone, and questioning how was I going to cope with this incredibly pressured, complex and dramatic change forced upon me. I was already struggling to stay afloat with life's challenges as it was.

My parents, Stojan and Dragica, along with my brother Levko, also known as Leo, and I, left Macedonia to start a new life in Australia when I was five years old. I started kindergarten in Sydney and I felt I had no voice, having difficulty expressing myself, as I only spoke Macedonian. My brother, however, was always there for me; he was my protector, teacher, advisor, and my best friend. Leo was older than me and adjusted better to the change, as he made friends easily. Both of my parents worked hard, long hours to get ahead in order to create a new life in a new country so we could buy a home and provide a stable foundation for us all.

In December of 1993, my family was delivered the unexpected and shocking news that Leo died in a tragic accident. He was only 34 years old, and whilst heading up the North Coast to pursue a job opportunity, he stopped for a swim at Newcastle's Nobby's Head beach, as it was a hot summer day. He was caught in a rip and drowned. His body washed up on the shore three days later. I was eight months pregnant with my first child and Leo's death was a shattering experience that left an immeasurable impact on us all. Although as a family we began to slowly deal with the huge void he left, Dad took it the worst, shutting down and checking out of life. We didn't know about the process of dealing with the grief and loss of death, especially of such a young person in our immediate family.

Leo was such a good hearted, fun loving and caring man, well-liked by all who knew him and loved by his family immensely; he was a strong, independent warrior who protected me, and now I had to learn how to not lean on him in my life. As we grew up I watched Leo and learned to be strong like him. Leo was always there when I needed him and I could rely on him. I could talk to him about anything; he was full of wisdom, ready to help me with any situation. I was very proud of the man I called my brother and cherish my memories with him. My heart breaks when I remember the fact that my three children won't get to experience what an awesome uncle they could have had. He was wise, and a great storyteller. He would have slipped in lots of life's lessons to his stories whilst watching them grow, guiding, mentoring and having fun with them.

I suffered from many nightmares after Leo's death. He kept coming and visiting me in my dreams, so real and vivid .. different scenarios, always saying something like, "What's going on? I'm not dead." The nightmares have faded over the years. I still cherish my memories. When I look back and reflect on my life with my brother, I realise how fortunate I was to have him be a part of my life, grow up with him, learn from him and have many cherished photos to look back on. I was lucky to have had such an inspiring man in my life who loved me unconditionally.

I had no idea how to navigate the next chapter of my life, now faced with the diagnosis of my dad, on my own, without my brother's love and support. How was I going to get through this? I was faced with a double whammy, as my marriage ended at the same time my dad became ill. I felt so alone .. my world was rocked to the core of my being. How was I going to support my dad, my mum, and my three young children all going through their own life processes and challenges?

I was working and studying at the same time, burning the candle at both ends .. trying to stay afloat, yet drowning. I was being pulled down by life's challenges and seemingly insurmountable circumstances. Although I felt like falling apart and letting go, I couldn't .. I had to find something to hang on to. There was no one there for my family if I fell apart. I was it. I was the one who had to be someone I never in my wildest dreams thought I could, or ever had to become. It was do or die, and dying was not an option as everyone was relying on me to get us all through, to be the glue, the one to hold it together. I had to step it up, find resources within myself I never knew existed. I had to go within and rely on higher powers to get us all through this extremely challenging change in our lives.

Taking it one day at a time allowed me to flow through and slowly learn to become stronger for myself and support my loved ones. I was in a state of uncertainty, with no time to study and fully understand the effects of Dementia. I was witnessing losing my dad slowly, however, I was going to learn all I could to help him. It was my chance to reciprocate for my Father being there for me my whole life. Watching my dad deteriorate was something I had no comparison in my life for, nor had anyone I knew had exposure to this type of experience. There was no one to help guide me or get advice. I had to learn, explore and discover how to make life bearable for all of us, still creating joyful moments whilst we were traveling this road. We were all in this together. It was affecting all of us slowly and surely. I came across a quote and I decided to apply it: "What does not kill me only makes me stronger."

Reflecting on my dad's diagnosis at the time of his passing encompassed five years of struggle, meltdowns, breakdowns and breakthroughs, and was my biggest journey of growth ever undertaken, by choice. During those years I couldn't stick my head in the sand like an emu and pretend it wasn't happening, although there were many times I wanted to run away and hide but there was nowhere I could escape my pain. I had to face it and deal with it one day at a time. Balance is what I needed in my life and I looked deep within myself to provide that for me and my family. I questioned myself on how I could stay afloat and not drown completely.

I started to explore my options by reading lots of books whenever I could. I also researched the internet for information on Dementia and care every moment I had. I bought myself an iPod, invested in audiobooks to listen to whilst I was on my own and began to expand my mind, to better myself for my family. I started reading motivational books to find a way to experience pleasurable moments through the pain I was living in. I needed to learn to get some clarity amidst the confusion in my mind whilst grasping for breath through my frustrations.

A switch was turned on inside of me, I consciously decided to become a student of life, although I was an avid reader, from my mid-twenties I became interested in personal growth, I enjoyed growing and learning. However now, faced with this situation my mind opened up and I started to become like a sponge, thirsty and hungry for information. I enrolled my children in a pilot program at their Primary School called Seasons of Growth. The program was designed to teach the students attending about the seasons of change with any grief and loss they may face. It was highly beneficial to my children and I learned through them, as they shared their learnings and experience's of the workshop. Through the workbooks we were exploring together I realised that I had to take a break from studying as I was burning the candle at both ends. I decided to defer my studies to focus on my family as working and studying was failing me. I had to start taking my dad to his medical appointments, manage my family and my parents lives as well.

Throughout my life's challenges and on a road of personal development there were a few books that resonated and assisted me immensely; one that stood out as I found it inspiring was The 7 Habits of Highly Effective People by Stephen Covey. This book is full of wisdom and one of the seven habits is to: "Sharpen the Saw" which means preserving and enhancing the greatest asset you have which is you. It means having a balanced program for self-renewal in the four areas of your life. In order to develop our character, there are four dimensions in our lives that need attention: physical, mental, social/emotional and spiritual.

Examples of activities that can expand our Spiritual dimension could be: Spending time in nature, expanding you're spiritual self through meditation, music, art, prayer or service, renewing yourself in each of the four areas creates growth and change in our lives. Having read this book in 1994 this was the year and the point where my conscious spiritual journey started, practicing all the examples just mentioned along with my own character development in all four dimensions. I needed to grow in my line of work to be highly effective assisting my clients with their struggles in life, I needed to apply these habits, to seek to understand, to be empathetic and be able to see the world from my client's perspective.

I referred to this book and many others throughout my life. Books were like my best friends; if I found myself struggling or being challenged, I would walk over to my bookshelf and pick up a book, I had books on every area of life's challenges. If I was stuck, I would read a book and gain someone else's insights and perspective and open my mind to another point of view. I had to build my character and become another version of myself, a wiser version, because I believed that when we are faced with a situation that's challenging, we can see it as an opportunity to expand and evolve, it's a process, to sharpen the saw to overcome and learn from the challenge. In my experience everything in life is a process, we live in a process orientated world. Having supportive, loving and positive friends along with motivational and soul soothing music are great aids to assist our growth in becoming evolved human beings connected to our hearts and our spirits.

During this stage of my life, I was hungry for information on what could help me understand what my dad was going through and how I could be of service, I researched as much as I could. According to Alzheimer's Australia Dementia describes a collection of symptoms that are caused by disorders affecting the brain, it is not one specific disease. Dementia affects thinking, behaviour and the ability to perform everyday tasks. Brain function is affected enough to interfere with the person's normal social or working life. People from their forties onwards can have dementia although it is more common over the age of sixty-five. Knowledge and information are key. When we learn, we grow and we can help others and ourselves – this was a phase in my life of enormous growth. Alzheimer's Australia has a website with help sheets, advice, common sense approaches and practical strategies on the issues most commonly raised about dementia. They also have a contact telephone number listed for further assistance and help, which is a great resource to have if faced with a similar situation as mine.

Trying to make sense of my dad's stage of life, I expanded my reading scope and according to a book on 'Death and Dying' by psychiatrist Elisabeth Kubler-Ross. Losing a parent, spouse, or other loved one's is a really hard process to deal with. But what most of us don't know, is that until it happens, it hurts for a long time, as death my dementia, is a slow process. According to experts, there are recognizable stages or signposts that you'll pass through as you move from bereavement to healing. Kubler-Ross popularized the idea of the five stages of grief. Since then some experts have continued to work with Kubler-Ross's model, while others have simplified the theory to include just three or four stages, or expanded the list to as many as ten.

Most experts agree that everyone processes a loss by experiencing a series of different feelings, though we may go through these stages in a different order or skip one altogether. There are guides that explain the stages of grief and how to navigate them to find comfort and healing. Further information is available through books and on computers via the internet; if we don't have a computer or internet our libraries have these services in Australia. We can do our own research, find the information we require and put into practice to help ourselves and our loved ones.

Assisting in the care of my dad, I realised I needed help to navigate the health care system and I couldn't do it on my own, struggling with responsibilities both my own and my families, if I didn't reach out and get the help I needed, I was going under. Too tired to just keep my head above water on my own without a float, and apart from attending seminars on Dementia, reading all the self-development books that came across my path I realised I needed external professional help. I found assistance that was provided in our health care system here in Australia. The A.C.A.T (Aged Care and Assessment Team) were brilliant in providing information, assistance and guidance throughout my personal struggles and I am forever grateful. We are very fortunate here in Australia to have the health care system that we do as many other countries, unfortunately, lack that support.

I would often find myself sitting with my own thoughts in my head and it wasn't getting me anywhere, constantly looping, thinking, crying, and riding the emotional rollercoaster of life. I had to remind myself to reach out to get help, processing my grief was not an easy task to achieve on my own, realising I don't have to do it on my own and I wasn't supposed to do it on my own was a breakthrough for me. I had to get out of my head and reach out as there are lots of resources available. I have learned that when we as human beings are faced with situations that we view as problems, we have the power to change our thinking and we can shift our mindsets to thinking challenges instead of problems. Adversities can and do build inner strength if we view them as opportunities. If we were to connect and open our hearts and come from a place of love and service to others, we can achieve amazing results helping and assisting each other in our journey. When we share our stories, trials and tribulations of our challenging situations and how we have learned and grown, then other people who may be facing similar situations can grow in the process of the sharing. If I had reached out earlier and allowed help and guidance in when I was faced with my own divine storm, it may have been a much smoother transition. However, that was not my case I had to learn and investigate on my own, which is why I chose to share my story to help and assist others in their journeys of life.

It was my choice stay open, to learn and grow through my challenge I had been faced with, and I was open to being assisted in anyway shape or form. One day I was having a chat with a friend and their partner at a birthday party, they shared their experience of a recent weekend seminar they attended at Landmark Education. The seminar had made a huge difference in their lives, they shared the benefits of how it left them feeling free to express themselves to each other from a real and authentic space. I was captivated by their experience and our conversation, it had left me feeling intrigued, therefore I wanted to learn more about their experience and gifts they had uncovered within themselves. I was advised about a special evening that was available every month to experience an introductory session and I was invited to attend. I was so confused and frustrated with my situation I had so much going on in my head, I had to make some sense of my world, I wanted what they had, clarity and a sense of freedom that I was looking for at that stage of my life.

I attended the free evening introductory session and I found the experience thought-provoking, my mind had shifted and opened up to possibilities that were available to me by attending the Forum, in which I registered on the evening. I attended the next scheduled weekend, immersed myself fully in freeing my mind and my negative thinking, therefore I gained clarity and a sense of freedom to express myself in my relationships that I hand not experienced before. During the weekend seminar I made a call to my dad to tell him how much I loved and appreciated him, he was always there for me he was a truly amazing and wonderful father and I was able to express my gratitude for his unconditional love and presence in my life. That conversation had my whole world shift for the better; I was left free to be open and loving in my relationships with my family and in my life.

When we are born we have a life cycle, unfortunately, most of us live as if we will be here in physical form forever, not stopping to smell the roses, constantly running, doing or chasing the next big thing that we think will make us happy. Through my journey I have learned to accept life more, the importance of accepting instead of resisting and fighting it, being able to accept and just be with it. I struggled with my dad's deterioration, I fought hard to help him, to assist him to extend his life, and I just couldn't give up. I wasn't able to accept he was dying and deteriorating, for the life of me I just couldn't accept he wasn't going to be around forever. This was the hardest situation for me to accept, the most painful in my life I have ever had to encounter. When my brother passed, it was instant and we had to learn to live without him. With my dad, I knew in advance that his mind and body were shutting down and preparing to leave the physical plane and I would not ever see him again. I didn't like what was happening, I did accept it and just went on with the process doing the best I could.

I learned to cherish the time we had left, as hard as it was watching my dad's mind shut down I felt so helpless, I felt so angry and sad, I was in excruciating pain watching him. His mind fading away, losing parts of his mind and his memory. The times when he would forget who we were and couldn't recall where he was, were the most painful. Mum and I chose to take care of him at home, he wanted to be with us even though he couldn't remember us sometimes, there were times we needed respite and to remember ourselves. As we were struggling to take care of him at home and if I could do it all again, I wouldn't change a thing. That time was important for us to be with him the best we could, and when he was in respite care we missed him terribly. But we needed the break and to recover with our own health as best as we could to continue the journey and battle we were fighting. We were learning to cherish the moments we had together, creating memories along the way to the end.

Five years from my dad's diagnosis to the end of his life, five years of learning, battling, suffering and growing in the process. It's true, experiences do shape us, they do help us have thicker skin, to cope better with life's challenges and learning to experience moments of joy in the pain and seeking clarity in the confusion wasn't an easy task. To flow through a situation or event and become someone we thought we could never be, we never had to be, until faced head on with this circumstance. This can break us or make us become resilient, as adversities can build resilience through how we look at the situation. It depends on which way we shift our perspective. Is it working for us or against us? And do we have open hearts to love? We all have the choice to become bitter or better through life's events.

One evening I found myself reflecting in thought, I sat with myself and I decided to do a funeral exercise, to design and write my own headstone. I projected forward and envisioned my own death, and I asked myself, what do I want to be remembered for? I looked deep within, reflected on my life's challenges and what I was being faced with now with my dad's life almost nearing the end. I wrote what I wanted to be remembered for. I wanted to be remembered for being thought provoking and inspiring to others in life. In that exercise I realised I had to become that which I wanted to be remembered for, I had to become inspiring, to be able to touch people's hearts and help them think positive and loving thoughts. I learned that it had to start with me. I had to think positive and inspire myself to get through my challenge, to come out of it as best as I could, I had my family to think about who were also traveling this journey with me, we were all in it together, I was the glue, keeping it intact to get us through.

My dad passed away one evening just after I had left the hospital. He had been in the hospital for a number of weeks, I watched his body shut down, the doctors did all that they could for him. We did all that we could do for him. Dad's swallowing mechanism failed and he was getting pneumonia, we couldn't have him fed by the drip for the rest of his life. Our only other option was to have surgery and open up a whole in his stomach and feed him through a tube, his last quality of life had gone, the enjoyment of food, he couldn't remember anyone anymore, he couldn't walk or talk, he laid in bed silently breathing. The doctors decided against the operation as this could make matters worse, dad had no quality of life left to enjoy we had to let him go, let his body shut down, and so it did slowly.

One evening after I left the hospital to head back and manage the functions of home life, dinner, homework etc… within a couple of hours of being home I got the call. Dad had passed away, and I wasn't there for him, I wanted to hold his hand as he took his last breath and I physically wasn't able to be in two places at one time. When he died, a part of me died also, I was beside myself. My world went dark, my mind went into shock, my body numbed now that he left life. I was devastated and at the same time at peace. He was no longer in pain, that's the only thing I could think about. The five-year battle had come to an end for him and for us. Although it was nearly midnight, my emotions were soaring but it dawned on me that the battle was over, dad was at peace, and I lost my Hero.

During the funeral arrangements, my mind was feeling foggy and cloudy. I felt bogged down like I was carrying the weight of the world on my shoulders, heaviness and fatigue took over my existence and I barely coped with it all. I was walking through a dark tunnel of the unknown again whilst coping with the grief and loss of dad, my body almost shut down in order to cope with the stress levels. We chose a funeral home and followed their guidance and support, we were able to organise the viewing and were lovingly supported by our relatives and friends.

The day of the funeral was during our Easter, the second worst day of my life, living through my brother's death and now trying to get through my dad's funeral was a catastrophically life shifting event for my family. Things just couldn't get any worse than what they already were. The weather was dark and stormy, it was pouring rain, and it was horrible. I don't think I slept much that night and if I did it was restless tossing and turning for a couple of hours. Trying to hold it all together at the funeral service was not working for me; tears were streaming down my face on their own, no matter how hard I tried to be strong and hold myself together.

I was in emotional turmoil, taken over by extreme sadness and pain whilst looking at dad lying in his casket. Writing this chapter has been a difficult task, going back to the past, reliving and recalling these memories in order to write about it has been extremely challenging and somewhat healing at the same time. Reflecting and revisiting old memories, stored emotions and blocks has been like opening up a can of worms for me to deal with all over again, to write about the past, to share my experience with the readers has been daunting. As I look back I also remember the love and support from family and relatives. We all felt loved and supported throughout the day of the funeral and ended it with the wake in my father's honour. That's what I remember, the love, the support we experienced at both my father's and my brother's funerals. They were my hero's, they are loved, cherished and remembered always by my family, we honour them both in our hearts and always will.

In my own experience of life, I have learned that it's the journey that matters, not the destination. On my roller coaster of emotions that I have lived and experienced, I have also learned to deal with myself and my own emotions more effectively given my challenges. Living through losing my dad and my brother, developing myself in the process, has helped me become more present and loving. In August 2015 my youngest daughter, Tiana, and I took my mum overseas to Macedonia to visit family and for mum to see her sister as it had been over 10 years since they last saw each other. My auntie wasn't well and was living with the last stages of Dementia.

Tiana had never been to Macedonia, and I hadn't been back since I was 13 years of age. With sadness in our hearts, we were only there for a few weeks. It was a call of duty for me, to take mum to see her sister for the last time, the last goodbye it was the last time that we were going to see my auntie. Again my emotions exploded within, I felt the duality of happiness to see everyone and the sadness we were faced with.

However, given my life's experience, I was better able to handle the situation knowing we are all going to pass on at some stage of our life. Not a good thought and definitely not a good feeling, but it's a fact. Facing the pain of loss again, I was somehow able to find, see and experience joy in the moment.

We were able to explore Slepce and Demir Hisar, visit some of mum's old friends, relatives, and the Monastery. Slepce is a beautiful village in Macedonia where I was born and lived till I was 5 years old. I saw the trip as an opportunity to create treasured memories we will cherish for life. Whilst in Macedonia we managed to experience some of its unbelievable beauty and culture with our relatives. I was in awe as the country has countless beautiful mountains, pristine national parks, exquisite lakes and incredible monasteries. With so many things to see and do, the people we met along the way were friendly and warm. The country and its atmosphere were amazing. Macedonia has a rich, colourful and inviting feel to it. Having been born there I was happy to explore it with Tiana and my mother. I'm looking forward to going back hopefully in the near future and exploring more with my family.

IN SUMMARY:

I was invited by John Spender to share my story to assist other people who may be experiencing similar situations on their journey.

When faced with life's challenges we need to be compassionate for ourselves as well as our loved ones, and realise we can somehow get through it. By tapping into our inner resources and reaching out for help and guidance. Knowing another person has experienced a similar situation, we trust that they understand us.

Reflecting back on my life's journey I have learned to build resiliency through facing life's adversities with love and gratitude. My breakdowns became breakthroughs when I shifted my perception of my struggles into challenges and grew from them. This has allowed me to experience moments of joy as I work through everything I am faced with at any point in time. I sometimes recite the Serenity Prayer at night and keep a gratitude list. I add to it before I go to bed as part of my evening routine .. this practice reminds me of how grateful I am to still be alive and cherish my loved ones, and to experience joy and calm before I drift off to sleep.

I have worked in the Community Services field for almost twenty years. I have completed my Diploma in Community Services, passing with high distinctions. I have counselled, case managed, supported, guided and assisted clients with change and transformations in their own lives throughout my career. Providing support to another is what I love doing and being of service to assist them in becoming better versions of themselves brings me joy. Given my many years of work experience, endless hours of on-the-job and in-house training, as well as attending countless motivational and personal growth seminars throughout my life. I am able to assist those wanting or needing change to master their own lives effectively. Learning how to enjoy the process of change, regardless of what you're dealing with, can be extraordinarily challenging. I know I have the skills to coach and mentor those needing assistance gaining a positive perspective throughout life's curve balls.

I welcome all opportunities that arise in the future, as my legacy is to help with what I can impart from my experience .. to assist in every way I can to contribute to humanity shifting its consciousness to love and asking what's possible. I am available to counsel and guide clients to attain their potential and mastering their unique journeys more effectively.

I am available to speak at events, support groups, and workshops. I can be contacted at theartofbecomingresilient@gmail.com

"Choose your beliefs and the words you speak wisely, as they do create your reality."

~ Katrina Gulabovski

www.theartofbecomingresilient.com

Chapter 10

Finding Your Purpose

By Dario Cucci

During most of my life I was looking to learn more about my own purpose. For some reason I felt that I was destined to be an actor because I loved performing and moving people emotionally with the power of story. When I moved from Switzerland to Australia in my mid-twenties I decided that this was going to be my mission, to see if being an actor is really what I wanted to do with my life and find out if it was my purpose.

Well things turned out a bit different than expected, first I worked in the retail and hospitality industry, I also sold supplements and at night worked in bars. This was not really what I had in mind but I thought it was just the beginning of my life in Australia, and I was right. After my first few years I studied and trained to become a personal trainer. I successfully qualified to be able to work in this field. Soon after I got offered to work as a franchisee within Fitness First and ended up, during my 5 years working as a personal trainer and mentoring apprentice personal trainers. I ended up doing really well but I felt that it wasn't enough. Next to my personal training I also continued my hobby to become an actor, studying at the Actors Pulse in Sydney for almost 5 years. I decided that I didn't want to continue going there after I felt betrayed by my acting teacher and mentor for embarrassing me in front of my fellow acting students.

Let's go back to my career, so after I stopped working as a personal trainer, I studied and became a Neuro Linguistic Programming (NLP) Practitioner and NLP Master Practitioner and started working as a NLP Coach. I did well with this but felt kind of lonely and there was no consistency in income. Soon I looked for another job and got offered to work on commission only as a salesperson, selling Anthony Robbins programs and tickets in Australia with Empowernet. At first I thought it was going to be easy, because when I did sales as a personal trainer and NLP Coach by selling my own Services, I never had an issue and did really well. But in the new position I was doing it mostly over the phone, so I didn't see the person I was talking to and it was a different kind of selling than when I did it face to face.

After 2 weeks of struggling I finally had a breakthrough after 2 weeks of making a lot of cold calling phone calls. There was a mixture of some existing inactive customer phone calls, which you could call warm leads but they were not really warm because they had not been called in almost a year. If you have a customer that once purchased and then you don't talk to them within 1 year it ends up being a cold lead just like the ones you get from Facebook or Google advertising, because you need to re-establish a relationship with them.

Anyway, back to my breakthrough, I got up in the morning after 2 weeks of struggling and I made the decision right then and there, if I don't make 1 sale today I will quit this job. I went into the office, looked through the CRM (Client Relationship Management System) the company used, "Salesforce", and I ended up calling a customer that bought an Unleash the Power Within ticket and attended the event a couple of years back. I had a great conversation and she expressed interest at coming to the next Date with Destiny Event that was to be held 6 months down the track.

So I did a follow up call and spoke with her again about the event, this time instead of me focusing on just selling, I actually got to know her a bit. I answered all her questions and voila I made my first sale and got my first commission paid of $1000. From then on things looked up. Over the coming months I did very well within the company and made additional sales revenue of over 1 million dollars during my time with them, which was just short of 12 months.

But things came to an end when Anthony Robbins decided to take a break from visiting Australia. My Supervisor, Saira, felt bad that I wasn't offered a permanent position. The CEO of the Company had someone new in mind and didn't want to offer me a full-time position. He was okay with me being on commission only but that's as far as he was willing to have me working for his company. Saira always had my back and she appreciated the work I did for the company. She had a contact that owned an events company called "Universal Events" which held NLP training courses. Not just those where one gets qualified to be an NLP Practitioner but also NLP events for the public where strategies were taught to them to achieve their lifestyle and business dreams.

I remember that I ended up getting a call from the owner of the company on my birthday after Saira put in a good word for me and I sent my CV to her. So on my Birthday I get this phone call, we talked for about 30 minutes and after she offered me the job right on the spot, I was super happy about that.

By the way my Birthday is 23 April 1971 if you would like to send me a present ;) .

That is how I got my next job working in sales and my career went up. Not only did I work in sales on the phone but I also assisted training the crew at the live events the company held in Australia and New Zealand. I gave the management team input on what can be implemented to increase sales revenue after an event took place.

Again I did really well, and I also learned a lot from the coaching that the company provided at the events. I was lucky enough to attend the events for free due to the hard work I put in and the great results that I got from it. On average I made an additional monthly sales revenue of about $150,000, before I started working there the average month with the other salesperson was about $50,000 a month. But after I started we both were motivated and supported each other at doing well, so we both stepped it up and on a great month we would achieve each about $100,000 to $150,000 in additional sales revenue for the company.

But not everything that seems perfect from the outside was perfect. With each and every company I worked with I found it was stressful because of the lack of appreciation they had for salespeople and the lack of admin organisation they had in place for clear internal communication with the team as well as with the customers. As I moved on to work with other companies over the years I witnessed and experienced a lot of what I feel was corruption and bad management on building a business. As a result a lot of great people I knew working in sales, customer service and marketing had to quit because it became unbearable. Things like misleading sales promises where the sales team, including myself, were told one thing to mention to the customer but then 3 days later the company went back on that and changed the rules about it. So we then had to talk to those customers again and let them know about the changes, some of which of course became upset because they were told one thing but then it turned out to be something else. I then had to do damage control and look at solving it, to make it right for the customer but also do what was asked of me by the management of the company.

Sometimes that worked, but a lot of times I felt very angry with the owner and the management because of their lack of admin setup and non-transparent communication that was going on within the company structure. Where, for example, we would tell the customer the special offer that we were offering on the phone is not available to the public and is the best offer, only to see that the marketing department the very next day promoted a better offer than we had.

That made the company look insincere and made me as the salesperson look stupid, like I was lying to the customers I spoke to. This made me furious and this is just one of the many examples of what I could tell you about bad internal communication structures that lead companies to get a bad reputation whilst also losing great people that worked for them.

In my 15th year working for companies, training salespeople but also still selling other people's products and services I ended up getting to a point of no return. For months on end I felt very frustrated, angry and stuck, unable to do anything about it. Then one day during my lunch time I felt my face changing. At first I had a cramp and then all of a sudden I had no feeling whatsoever, it felt weird. I looked in the mirror and saw that one side of my face was not moving at all, it was dropping down and my speech was blurry at best. I was afraid that I was having a stroke due to the stress I had over the past few months and the unhealthy lifestyle I lived, by eating unhealthy foods.

I went to my manager and within minutes of telling him they called an Ambulance and I was driven off to the Hospital nearby. I was in the Hospital for about 3 hours, during which they asked me several questions, ran a brain scan to see if I did have a Stroke or if it was something else. After the 3 hours the doctor told me "You have Bells Palsy", they gave me some anti-inflammatory medication to get the cells that were inflamed down, allowing them to heal a bit and told me that once I ran out I should go to visit my doctor to get another prescription.

Believe me, those 3 hours felt like the longest hours of my life, not only that but it got me asking myself the question "Did I really make the most out of my life and if I were to die today, would I be okay with it?" A tough question to ask, because the answer I got was "No, you are just in the beginning and you have not lived nor found your purpose yet".

So back home I ended up still coaching one of my clients via Skype. I didn't want to just give up and was determined to get better, I was able to talk but it was kind of unclear and blurry, so I had to slow down the speed at which I spoke for people to understand me. When I ran out of the medication, I ended up going to the doctor to find out what else can be done to speed up the healing process of Bells Palsy besides the medication I was given. I don't like pills and medications, and unless I really need it, I prefer the alternative way and eastern medicine.

Anyway, so there I am in the doctor's office, the doctor himself was overweight, unhappy and resigned to the life he created, in one word "Boring". He looked at me, looked at the medical description I brought with me that I got from the hospital and then said "So what do you want me to do?" I told him I needed to get my prescription refilled, enough medication for another 7 days, he told me "sure, but then after this batch of medication, you will need to stop with it". I was fine with that, so I wanted to know what else could be done to speed up the healing process of my face once I stopped taking the pills?

His answer "There is nothing you can do, just wait and see if time heals it".

I couldn't believe he just said that! Inside of me I felt angry and I thought to myself I am going to prove you wrong, you bastard of a freaking doctor, who the fuck are you to tell me that there is nothing that can be done!

So I did my own research online and found out several things that can be done about it, one of which is acupuncture. I took it upon myself to see an acupuncture therapist and the first thing she said when she met me was "You look very angry". Oh yeah I was very angry, any surprise there, I think not. But she was very nice, she comforted me and gave me hope to believe that something can be done. The therapy room was nice, very relaxing and in the background was calm meditation music.

The acupuncture therapy I did worked. In the first 2 Months I went every week twice a week, then as things started to improve with my face I continued with it once a week and eventually after 6 months only once every fortnight. I decided to also improve my diet, to stress less about things I could not control and kept doing self development trainings to find my own purpose. After a while I decided that I couldn't find and be living my purpose whilst being far away from my family, which most of them lived in Switzerland. So I moved from Australia back to Switzerland and there the healing process continued. My Mum is an Energy Healer and some of the techniques that she used with me to help heal my Bells Palsy made a big difference.

I believe that one can have a good career, be healthy, have great friends and good financial success all at the same time and I didn't want to be living a life alone on my own just to accomplish myself with my career. Within 2 years of being back in Switzerland, not only has my Bells Palsy now healed by about 95% but I was able to start my own company "On-Call-Business Ltd" and within the first 2 months of starting it, I had already my first 3 private business clients that I worked with. My aim and purpose in my Life now is to inspire and teach other business owners how to avoid making the mistakes that the companies I worked for made, which at times even cost them their reputation and occasionally had to close the business because of it.

To summerize it all up on what I want to tell you with this story; don't follow the crowd and what others tell you is possible or not. Just because western medicine has no answers to Bells Palsy and how to heal it or know where it comes from, that does not mean that there is no answer. Same goes for business, just because everyone is using automation to get leads and make sales online does not mean that this is the only way to build a business.

In fact the strategy that I teach my clients is the opposite of that, I teach them to re-engage with their clients to build a more impactful relationship which was one of the strategies I used in my career to be a very successful salesperson. So never give up on following your purpose and your dreams. Stand out from the crowd instead of doing what everyone else is doing in your situation. If I listened to the Doctor, my face would not have healed to 95% by now. Believe me, it took courage and determination to go against what he said but in my eyes I had nothing to lose and everything to win.

I see the same pattern with clients I take on board, they're tried with everything in internet marketing, cold calling and so on, until they come and see me. I then tell them what they can do to optimize their business, I start working with them and within their first 4 weeks of working with me, they experience a major improvement, whereas before they did everything everyone else did in business, only to fail and lose money with it. The marketing consultant that I spoke with on Skype after I had my Bells Palsy incident and got home from the Hospital, she struggled to convert her leads that she got online into clients. After my conversation with her and the implementation of the Fast Track Sales System Strategy I taught her, she went from having 1 new client a month to 5 new clients in one week.

I am just telling you this so that you can be inspired to find your way in business as well as in life because "Life is short so let's make the most out of it and live it with purpose".

I can tell you with confidence that I found my purpose and I love what I do. Now I am in much healthier shape, my face is almost completely healed and I own my own company and do what I love doing.

Here is my purpose in one sentence: I have been born to inspire, teach and coach people around the world to rise above average and achieve excellence in their business and life.

So what I do these days is that I hold seminars and do 1 on 1 consulting and coaching to make sure that business owners implement powerful communication strategies internally within the business to lead their teams, and externally use transparent communication strategies to build better relationships with their customers. When you do the right thing by your customer and lead your employees by being the role model you want them to become, there won't be any limit to what you can achieve with your business and best of all, you will never have to spend money on advertising again as you continue getting referrals from your customers due to your customer service. This is for all kinds of business sizes no matter if they are a one man business or SME business with 5 - 100 Employees.

If you are an entrepreneur or a business owner that wants to optimize your admin and communication structure to serve your customers better but also to increase your sales by 300% by implementing powerful communication strategies, then hit me up for a first time free 20 minute discovery and solution call on Skype. During this call I will point out to you which areas in your business needs improvement when it comes to communication and admin.

At the end I will talk to you about what needs to happen to get the results you are after and then if I can contribute value by helping you make that happen, I will make you an offer to work together with me to take your business to another level.

Visit my website to book a call Sales Breakthrough Session Call with me Valued at $250 for FREE www.dariocucci.com.

Chapter 11

It's Never Too Late

By Marina Marsden

When John Spender first approached me to write my story, I honestly thought he was kidding. "No Marina, this is real." Like seriously. Never in a million years did I think anybody would be interested in my humble story, but here goes…

Epiphany

At the age of 8 during a thunderstorm, I looked up and watched in awe as the lightning illuminated the whole night sky, momentarily turning night into day with a blast of white light. As I gazed on, I noticed the sky had become unusually red and my heart started to beat rapidly. Suddenly tears flowed from my eyes as I was choked with emotions, feeling scared and fearing that the world was about to end. I quickly closed my eyes, asking God for forgiveness and prayed for the safety of my family. As I waited for the end to come, I imagined tornadoes whisking me away and destroying the world that I knew. My imagination was running wild as I awaited imminent punishment.

After a few minutes of chanting prayers, I slowly opened my eyes and realised that my fears were unfounded. As I looked up again towards the fiery red sky, I was feeling calmer but quickly walked away from the window to my room where I buried my head under the pillow. Feeling somewhat relieved, I pledged to be a better daughter as I cried myself to sleep.

A few days earlier, my parents had bought me an expensive dress to wear during a function that we were attending. Although I had liked the dress in the store, I later decided that I did not like the dress and refused to wear it, causing distress to my mum – such a brat I was!

Family Life

I was second born into a family of six. My dad was a site supervisor for a Japanese construction company and my mum was a full time housewife, originally from Indonesia. I have a brother, Rizal, who is a year older than me and like most siblings do, we fought a lot. My sister, Marini, was born 4 years after me. Dad was always busy working, even on weekends, so mum was left to take care of me and my siblings. Financially we were doing quite well. During dad's off day, he would take us to our favourite places, MacDonald's, amusement rides, play bowling and shopping at big malls. Back in the late 80s, it was considered quite a big deal. At least to me.

As our family grew, mum started to do child-minding to make some additional income for our family. Our neighbour from the 4th floor would send their cute new-born to our place every morning before going to work and would collect him back only in the evening, 5 days a week for 2 ½ years.

When my youngest brother Faddly was born in 1993 things had started to change for us. Dad was declared bankrupt after being a guarantor for a 'friend' whom had run away and left him in the lurch, leaving my Dad struggling to make repayments. I remembered hearing my parents having arguments. It was a nightmare for all of us as there were lots of unpaid bills and Dad was the sole provider for the family. There were even times when we lived in darkness because of unpaid electricity bills. I felt helpless as I wasn't able to help my family's predicament but thankfully it did not affect my Primary School leaving examination results.

> *"School is like a lollipop. It sucks until it is gone"*
>
> ~ unknown

I don't have fond memories of adolescence life. Unlike primary school, the vibes at Secondary School were different. It seemed like there was a hierarchy and being accepted as part of a clique was crucial for survival. If you carried certain types of branded items like a Sonia Rykiel bag or Jean Paul Gaultier wallet, you're being looked upon. But for me? Just a sporty Umbro backpack. Initially it didn't affect me but as time passed, I did feel pressured especially when friends talked about things they had planned to buy or just to hang out after school. With only sufficient money for lunch at school, I usually declined meeting friends after school with excuses like having to take care of younger siblings who were 9 and 2 years old at that time. Mum had taken up her first job as a night operator, after having been a housewife for 13 years. It was tough initially, but we managed somehow. We usually spend weekends at home to save money. Academically, I was doing fairly well in school.

I had my first crush on a Chinese classmate towards the end of the year and was treated to my first cinema experience. However, during the movie, I was surprised when he politely broke up with me citing religious differences. He's a Christian whereas I'm a Muslim. He explained that his aunty had given him the advice prior to meeting me. I was taken aback at that moment but was trying to act cool but inside feeling so dejected. When school re-opened, we were still classmates and there was no awkwardness between us. We were both very young and never really knew what love was.

Later that year, I had my first part time job at a reputable Regent Hotel hanging baubles and gluing ornaments on a Christmas tree, together with three other school friends. We had gotten the job through one of our classmate's mum whom worked there as a florist. The job lasted for just 3 days but it was a great experience, earning me my first pay cheque of $85. I remembered giving my parents half of my earnings as we are taught in school about filial piety and to love and respect our parents. I believed that you get Barakah (divine blessings) especially when you share your wealth with your parents. It feels good to be able to contribute, albeit not much.

When I was in Upper secondary school, my dad got retrenched. The Japanese construction company that he had worked for ceased operation in Singapore. I remembered there were again unpaid bills on top of the debts that had already accumulated over the years and my dad had no choice but to borrow from his parents. Dad must have borrowed money one too many times because me and my siblings were branded as "anak orang miskin" (poor man's children) by my relatives and lots of snide remarks followed soon after. Some relatives would constantly compare me to my cousin Nura, whom I have been very close to since young, in terms of dressing up, boyfriends and even skin colour! Because I have an olive skin, I was made to feel like a 2nd class Malay citizen and my inferiority complex grew. All of the TV advertisements and magazines about skin whitening, slimming, breast enhancement and even an advert on getting taller did not help. I started to look at myself in the mirror with disgust. I hated my skin colour, nose shape, small chest, long feet and the list goes on. The only saving grace was that I was slim.

To make myself feel better, I saved my school lunch money to buy magazines instead. I would cut out those beauty enhancements and skin whitening adverts and compile them in a folder. In another folder I would paste cut outs of the branded bags that I desired. Flipping through those two folders gave me a sense of hope and provided me with a way to de-stress. It was almost therapeutic. I dreamt about saving up money to buy all the nice bags and undergo those beauty treatments. I even considered rhinoplasty which seems so superficial now. I started putting on an affordable compact powder to go to school and touching it up in between classes but still I wasn't satisfied with the way I looked.

Over the coming months I became more self-aware and wanted to improve my appearance. My school skirt became shorter and I tucked in my blouse more tightly. I still wasn't satisfied with the results and so decided on a bolder solution. I started to add clothes sponge inside my bra to make my breasts appear larger. It was a good feeling at first and I started to receive more attention, especially when I was wearing a bright coloured bra. That was until one day when I was noticed by a group of boys during a physical education lesson. Although I was unaware of it at the time, during the lesson I must have lowered my body enough whilst stretching for them to see through my t-shirt and that's where my nightmare begun. News of my additional padding had quickly spread amongst the boys. As I passed by my classroom, a boy from another class started to touch his chest, gesticulating and shouting "sponge breast" and laughing loudly. I was flustered. My cheeks were hot and red. My heart beat rapidly. I tried to control my tears. By then I knew that my classmates would have known about the drama. Thankfully, they had chosen to spare me the embarrassment. I was terrified and felt like the world was against me.

Due to that incident, I began to skip school as I couldn't handle the torment and bullying. I didn't confide in anybody, not even my closest friend. It was just too painfully embarrassing. My teachers seemed unaware of what had happened. It was my fault and I had brought it upon myself. I remembered crying in silence and never told anybody at home about the incident. I pretended like nothing had happened, even though deep down inside I was screaming for help. How would I have broached the subject, even if I had wanted to? I feared that I would have been scolded and punished for being an attention seeker.

I grew up in an environment where my parents didn't show outward emotions or give praise for my achievements. It's an Asian thing, even though they didn't say it, I knew that they love me and my siblings in their own way.

As a result, my grades suffered. I had begun to show less interest in academic studies and had taken on a part time job, three times weekly after school, as an accessories sales girl in town. Due to working, I would reach home at around midnight and then struggle to wake up for school the following day. I would arrive at school only around recess time which is around 3 hours after the 1st lesson had started. I would be brought to the discipline master's office and reprimanded on my punctuality.

Although I had tried to become more punctual, attending school had become more difficult following an accident at home. I had lost my footing and stumbled, falling badly on my left foot. Shortly afterwards I picked myself up and tried to walk. I could manage to walk a short distance by limping and at first I didn't believe that my injury was too serious. The following day I was supposed to take part in my school fashion parade, but after the fall I didn't feel like I would be able to participate. I called my classmate to explain what had happened. I planned to go to the doctor the following morning.

The next day as I woke up, I couldn't feel my left leg. It was a feeling that I hadn't experienced before. As I tried to sit up, I felt a shooting pain in my back and as I looked down at my feet, my left foot appeared to be twice the size of my right foot. Panic stricken, I bawled my eyes out causing my sister to wake up. She hurriedly called out to mum who had just returned from her night shift. Immediately, she called an ambulance and I was carried out on a stretcher.

After arriving at the hospital, we waited patiently to see the doctor. During that time, we had noticed that everybody around us was watching the news and talking about Princess Diana whom had sadly died due to an accident.

After some time, the doctor called us to his room and shared his diagnosis with us. He explained that my left foot bone was crushed and that I would be required to undergo surgery the next day. I wasn't scared at all when the doctor informed me that they would need to insert metal plates and screws into my bones and that I would be wearing a leg cast for the next 6 months. In fact, I was more interested to follow up on the Princess Diana story and looked forward to recuperating. It was somewhat of a relief that I wouldn't need to go back to school and face being ridiculed.

It was approaching the final year exam and I had fallen behind even further with my studies. I was struggling after my long absence from school. Feeling discouraged, I made excuses not to attend school, much to the displeasure of my mum. I hardly saw her during weekdays and as a result, we had started to drift apart.

Rumour has it…

There was a rumour going around school that a senior had a crush on me. "H" was a class monitor, a prefect and an athlete. He was quite well known amongst his peers and teachers due to his likeable personality. After all the unwanted attention that I received in the past, I blatantly ignored it. It was just a rumour and I never took it seriously. H did try to talk to me and passed on messages via classmates that he wants to get to know me. After a few months, we started talking on the phone and by the time the school term reopened in July, we were already an item. H was ever the gentleman, he would wait for me at the school bus stop and we walked to school together. He waited for me during recess time and bought me lunch every day. I wasn't sure whether he knew about the fiasco and even if he knew, he never once made me feel uncomfortable. Nobody dared to make fun of me in his presence. Still, I couldn't open up about my issues to him. I was putting on a façade, but deep inside, only God knew how I felt. But at the same time, being in a relationship with H made me want to fix the rift with my mum. We had a good talk and I was happy that we resolved our differences.

After finishing our final year exams, friends were discussing their future, ambitions and goals in life. But for me, I was clueless and never had any plans for the future. I didn't know who or what I wanted to be and didn't believe that I was good at anything. At that time, all I knew for sure was that I wanted to find a full time job and start to earn money to ensure a better life for my family. That's all I ever knew. I didn't want anybody to look down on my family anymore. All this while, my parents never coerced me into helping them out, I just wanted to help them on my own accord. I felt that deep sense of gratitude to them for bringing me up.

A few months later my exam results were out. I had a feeling I wasn't going to do well, given that the last 3 years of school had been an emotional rollercoaster ride. True enough, my grades weren't adequate to go to the college of my choice. H fared better than me as it was his 2nd time sitting the exam, as he had wanted to pursue college.

Good riddance school

Knowing that I was looking for work, my friend recommended me for a full time job as a receptionist at a family recreational club where most of the members were expats. She had been working there part time for a couple of months whilst we awaited our exam results. She had performed better in her exams and continued her studies in Brisbane. Meanwhile I was excited to replace her at the club and looked forward to starting my first full time job. It really felt like a new lease of life. I didn't miss school life at all. I was looking forward to earning a better salary and helping out my family.

Although I had no prior experience, I enjoyed working around friendly expats and their kids. It was such a breath of fresh air. I never failed to greet the members as they passed by my counter. I would ensure that I remembered their names and account numbers so that if they needed something I could take prompt action and get their details ready. I always took pride in my job.

Despite my enthusiasm, things were not always smooth sailing. One time a member started a conversation with me as they passed by the counter, there was nobody else in the vicinity at that time but yet I was later chided by my supervisor (let's call her 'S') for being too friendly. I couldn't understand her rationale as this was supposed to be a friendly club. Since I was only 17 at that time, perhaps she didn't believe that I was serious about my job. I had been informed by other colleagues and members that we had a huge turnover at the reception. People come and go and I had started to understand why.

Over the next few months, S started nit-picking over the smallest details. I had heard rumours that she had been bad mouthing me to other colleagues. I felt like I was being bullied again, just like I had at school. I remember her once calling me after leaving work to tell me that I hadn't placed a folder in the right compartment and asked me to return to work.

Despite the issues with S, I still enjoyed my job and persevered; although at times I considered resigning just as all the previous employees had. However, I doubted myself and questioned who would want to employ me. I had no working experience or paper qualifications. Going to work became a constant battle for me. I lost 8kg within 2 months due to work stress.

I worked mainly at night and on the weekend shift. This resulted in a strained relationship with H and soon after we separated. It was a terrible time for me, especially with the ongoing problems at work.

"God does not burden a soul beyond it can bear"

My prayers were answered. S was transferred to another department and I was relieved. Being financially independent gave me that sense of freedom and not having to rely on my parents.

My next supervisor (let's call her "J"), was nice to me initially, but that didn't last for long. Slowly she began to comment on all aspects of my work. She was a micro-manager and tried hard to find any small error, just so that she could correct me. She would openly compare my work performance with our newer colleagues. Feeling brave one day, I recall speaking up for myself but she dismissed me saying I was being argumentative. As she was more senior than me, I had to accept that she was right and remain obedient to her. This caused unnecessary anxiety; I would often self-reflect and question my self-worth. I really believed that I wasn't capable of anything but this job.

There was a constant cycle of thoughts, seemingly unescapable. I had wanted to stop the torture of my supervisors and believed that I couldn't do any better if I left the club. At the same time, I actually loved being the face of the club, working with the members and wanted to stay. Needless to say, I also needed the money.

> *"Sometimes the bad things that happen in our lives put us directly on the path to the best thing that will ever happen to us"*
>
> ~ Nicole Reed

Life had become routine, a constant cycle of work, home, sleep and repeat. The extent of my 'social life' consisted of relaxing with a colleague at the nearest coffee shop after work. It was at this time when I began to explore the online world, finding interesting people to chat with from abroad.

It was at this stage that I met Michael. Little did I know that he would change my outlook of life.

He came to Singapore 3 months after we first met online. Those 2 weeks that he was here, apart from sightseeing, we bonded well through conversation as we discussed the weather (Brits favourite topic of conversation), cultural diversity, aspiration and the future. I was soon attracted to his intelligence, demeanour and witty humour!

Unbeknownst to me, Michael had applied for a job in Singapore a week after he went back and decided to make a move here. It was almost unbelievable! Never would I have thought someone was willing to sacrifice his life to be closer to me. Feeling excited, I applied for 2 weeks leave to help him settle down in Singapore.

Work was draining me especially when I couldn't say no to overtime but reluctantly agreed to avoid further problems. However, the last straw came when J cancelled my leave few days prior to Michael's arrival. I was flabbergasted. All this while I've been a team player and dedicated to the company. I had done what I could to make a difference in the club. Understandably, I was disappointed.

> *'Pain doesn't just show up in our lives for no reason. It's a sign that something in our lives need to change'*
>
> ~ Mandy Hale

After almost 10 years working at the club and being in my comfort zone, I came to realise I wanted to make a change. I handed in my resignation letter directly to my HR and that very day happened to be my last day of work. Suddenly not having a job or income seemed pretty frightening. I was faced with an uncertain future but deep down, I knew I made the right decision. In hindsight, it was a blessing in disguise. I would have still been there now if not for that fateful day.

It was an exciting time full of changes.

Michael moved to Singapore 4 months later. I was happy to have him around but couldn't help feeling worried at times but he assured me things are going to be better. And this comes from someone who'd left his comfortable life and starting a new life thousands of miles away from home. I admire his guts. As I got to know him more, I realised how cool and laid back he is. The fast paced life unfazed him, he acclimatised to the heat and humidity shortly after and lived life simply. Inside my heart, I envy how uncomplicated his life is. He is like a breath of fresh air.

That slowly reshaped my perspective. By then I was convinced that it is completely up to us which direction we will take our life when changes approach.

Fresh start…

For the longest time I hadn't been comfortable in my own skin. Knowing Michael and later becoming his wife changed this. He helped me to rebuild my confidence. I became calmer and more patient. I learned to love myself again. I let my feelings out, my insecurities, my fears and mistakes. Most importantly, I learned to forgive my past self and to let go of my negative thoughts.

As I look back at my 8 years old self and recall my epiphany, I realised that I had already begun on my spiral of negativity during those moments when I had believed that my world was about to end. This downward spiral ended after I became strong in faith, surrounded myself with positive friends and removed myself from those toxic environments. The first step was to acknowledge and take action against my negativity, something that I had struggled with for many years.

I learned to rediscover myself and I know that each and every individual is special in their own ways. For the first time I believe that I am destined for bigger things in life.

New direction...

Two years ago I finally discovered what I wanted to do in life. It was something that I had loved to do since being young but never had the confidence to pursue until recently.

I first started when I was 10 years old, after observing my mum baking for a community function. The whiff of freshly baked cakes and cookies made me want to learn more. I would collect recipes from magazines and newspapers, cut them out and compile them in a book, just like I had collected those health and beauty enhancement cut-outs years later.

My passion for baking has been reignited. One day, I sat down flipping through my recipe collection. As I went through each page, ideas and inspirations sprang into my mind. Since I don't have formal training, I think a lot every time on planning and how I'm going to execute it. I started buying more baking utensils and ingredients and trying out new bakes every few days. Michael, being a desert person, is my biggest critic. Never one to sugar coat, he would give me constructive feedback on how I can improve on my bakes. It is all about trial and error. And patience. Especially in a hot kitchen. Whenever there are family birthday celebrations and friend meet ups, I would always take this opportunity to bake something new. From cakes to pastries and baking breads. Thanks to my family and a few good friends whom always gave me encouragement and have provided support. Baking helps me to release stress and feels almost therapeutic. I feel rejuvenated.

For this upcoming Christmas, I have received an order for 2000 pieces of personalised butter shortbread fingers from a corporate client. It was through word of mouth that they come to know about my shortbreads. This will be my biggest project to date yet and I am beyond thrilled!

The idea came last year when Michael's grandmother bought me a personalised stamp. Since both Michael and myself love buttery bakes,

I decided to make some with our names imprinted on it for our anniversary. When I posted the pictures on Facebook, it was so well liked that for the next few days my private messages were flooded with requests from friends and acquaintances wanting it as a gift. I was surprised by the overwhelming response but felt grateful that people loved my bakes and they could see how it would be extra special with their names on it.

With a new positive outlook on life, I have set new goals and look forward to new challenges. My ambition is to set up a home baking studio with private classes and high tea in the near future. I would love to share my love for baking and impart my knowledge from experience and share with people who have the same passion as I do. I would also like to help underprivileged kids and raise funds through baking. Many years ago I wouldn't have thought this possible but now, I have never been so certain as to what I want to do in my life. Suddenly, the future looks rosy.

Never be afraid to make a change. You'll be surprised at how it can transform your life.

Author Biographies

Chapter 1: John Spender

John started his first business at the age of 6 selling plaster of paris statues of Mickey Mouse and Donald Duck with his older brother. He later delivered pamphlets, papers, collecting trolleys, delivering milk and many other ventures all before he was 16. At 22 he had his own landscaping company completing council and government contracts, after giving up on that business due to an emotional break down.

John learnt the value of a balance life, of invested in systems and the power of developing people to do the work for you, while they and the business grow together. He sold his last business for a healthy profit and began learning and studying about personal development and coaching with his journey taking him all around the world and learning many different modalities. That led John to transition into Coaching and Mentoring where he has now help over a thousands of people from around the world to live a life of freedom, fun and passion. He created the "A Journey Of Riches" book series and he is currently making a movie/doco about the gift in adversity.

For more info visit www.ajourneyofriches.com

Chapter 2: Casey Plouffe

Casey Plouffe is a highly accomplished speaker, trainer, best selling author, and entrepreneur; currently one of the top income earners in an award winning, multi billion dollar health and wellness company. Casey discovered the power of gratitude and the secrets that rest inherent in one's own thoughts and feelings at a retreat in 2013. Upon returning home, Casey aligned herself with a deep purpose of helping others develop their own spiritual, emotional, physical, financial, and relational health after her own personal breakthrough. Through her challenges, trials, and tribulations, Casey has gained a new understanding of these experiences which she champions as the catalyst that has empowered her to fully embrace the blessings and successes she enjoys today. Casey is now committed to helping others learn how they too, can have unsurpassed financial and personal freedom through the power of self-awareness and unlocking their true potential.

Chapter 3: Marcia Miatke

Marcia is a management consultant and executive coach who is passionate about leadership and personal mastery. She partners with her clients to accelerate their personal and professional growth by focusing on their unique requirements for bringing out their inner leader. Her coaching aims to maximise the individual's performance and helps them push beyond their comfort zone to achieve the next level of success.

Marcia's diverse experience comprises Not-for-profits, Start-up Entrepreneurial Ventures, Sales and Marketing, and Higher Education. Her career included several roles in Higher education including Strategic Planning Manager at Curtin University where she played a key role in strategy, business analysis, industry and competitive intelligence and analysis. Previously, Marcia worked in marketing as a top performing business-to-business sales team leader.

In 2014 Marcia was awarded an Australian Postgraduate Award (APA) Scholarship to undertake her PhD research at the University of Western Australia. Her PhD focuses on the business areas she is most passionate about, Leadership and Change Management.

In 2011 Zonta International awarded her the Jane M Klausman Women in Business Award. Marcia earned a bachelor's degree in Management and Marketing and a first-class honours degree in Management from Curtin University.

Marcia lives in Perth Australia with her partner Ahmed and their three kids Adam, Lara and baby Aliyah.

Chapter 4: John Abbott

John Abbott, Audience Awakening Expert, Online Marketing Specialist, Lead Mentor for the Campaign Mastery Academy, co-author of the book "A Journey Of Riches, Making Changes" and the Creator of The Competition Gift and Profit Models.

In 2011 John and his wife Roz made the decision to relocate to Bali essentially to give themselves a better lifestyle and remove ourselves from "The Matrix". As a result, John has been able to work with and positively impact more entrepreneurs to make the change, and created a living environment that is ultimately free.

He contributes through B1G1 to great causes and gives his time to people on a purposeful mission. *"I get to spend such quality time with these amazing individuals, that they're like my extended family many who are attracted to live in our beautiful little village of Ubud on the Island of Bali"* John says with a big smile.

> *"My spiritual journey has been accelerated since arriving in Bali, and the energy, vibration and teachers who have been guided to me have influenced mine and my families life tremendously, and most of all we're looking forward to where this is leading us to and what lies ahead. Life's a journey, enjoy the ride!"*

~ John Abbott

Chapter 5: Goro Gupta

Goro Gupta is a passionate individual whose mission in life is to set people free form their financial shackles and get them on their path to creating true generational wealth.

Working with some big names directly, like Anthony Robbins, Arnold Schwarzenegger, Richard Branson, Tim Ferris and even Mark Bouris –

he has learnt quite a few lessons on how to live life to the fullest and the achieve mindset of the truly wealthy.

He also owns and manages 2 finance and mortgages broking firms as well as a property mentoring company teaching a select group of clients how to build a property empire of 10 properties in 10 years.

He started from humble beginnings where he could not attend school functions due to a lack of money. However, what he discovered on his journey to riches while creating passive income and accumulating over 25 properties will surprise you!

gorogupta.com

Chapter 6: Kiri Devi

Kiri Devi was born Joan Mudge in 1948, the youngest of six children growing up on a farm nestled beneath the Flinders Ranges in South Australia.

Joan was a teacher and Deputy Principal in Schools for over 40 years. She loves her 3 children, two grandchildren, family, and friends. The gift of life's challenging events has been a passion for studying Personal Development, Spirituality and Well-being. She is very grateful for many wonderful teachers and mentors.

While studying with Shanti Mission (Shanti a Sankrit word for Peace) Joan was given a Spiritual name, Kiri Devi which she is learning to grow into and contribute to raising awareness, consciousness and actions toward a sustainable, just and peaceful world for all.

Kiri Devi is currently continuing studies with Shanti Mission, The Robbins Madanes Center for Strategic Intervention, Authentic Education and creating a business, called "Understanding For Peace".

Chapter 7: Kelvin Kuan

In his former life, Kelvin Kuan was a marketing strategist and private consultant, working to sharpen brand differentiation, develop brand communication and promote brand identity. Having experienced a personal crisis of epic proportions, and over a period of recovery, he began to reevaluate his life goals and embrace change as a journey of personal discovery.

These days he lives somewhat off-the-grid while pursuing his interests in sustainable living, personal development, and community transformation.

If you believe that Kelvin can be of help to you, or what you are involved with, simply contact him at writekelvin@gmail.com and connect with him. Drop him a line too about how you may have benefitted from his chapter in this book. Start a conversation and stay committed towards positive personal change!

Chapter 8: Teresa Elliott

Teresa has overcome a decade of continuous trauma and has come out with flying colours. Now at 40 she is passionate about supporting people who suffer from Mental Health by Facilitating programs and being a Caseworker and Mentor for the last ten years.

Teresa is a mother of three beautiful children Hayden 9, Levi 6, and Maddison 4 with her husband Stuart. They live on the beautiful Central Coast in NSW Australia, just two hours north of Sydney.

Teresa is also a Reiki Energy Healer and on the path to transforming into an Urban Sharman. She is extremely passionate about the holistic approach to healing.

Teresa is Aboriginal, Maori and Mediterranean and raised in an Italian family. So she embraces culture!

Through 'gratitude' Teresa found her long lost brother overnight who was only a suburb away for 20 years from where she grew up.

Chapter 9: Katrina Gulabovski

Katrina lives in Sydney and works in the community service field. Passionate about making a difference in peoples' lives, inspired by unlocking human potential, helping and assisting others by guiding them in the art of becoming the best versions of themselves, master their emotions and assisting them to create possibilities to live a life they love.

Life is a game, if it's not working for us, we can level up and step it up. Problems can be turned into challenges to grow from and enjoy the process as life unfolds. As we evolve, it is a choice to begin making small shifts in perspective and creating possibilities to overcome those challenges. My legacy is to contribute to humanity and inspire others from my accomplishments and divine storms I have lived through my own life.

Chapter 10: Dario Cucci

Dario works with businesses to show them how to increase sales through building better relationships with their customers. Companies often waste thousands of pounds trying to find new customers only to lose them in the first 12 months with poor customer care.

Keeping a customer happy and loyal is much less costly than finding a new one and Dario teaches a simple and practical approach to building lifelong loyalty and long-term sales.

Dario first learned how to sell in his twenties when he made his living from 100% commission based selling with Anthony Robbins Events and over the next 15 years he has developed his own Relationship Sales System that teaches you how to build relationships that lead to sales and long-term loyalty.

Visit my website to get in touch with me to book a call on Skype www.dariocucci.com

Chapter 11: Marina Marsden

Marina was born in 1982 to a mixed parentage. Her mother is of Indonesian origin and her father is a Malay Singaporean. Growing up in Singapore, she had a comfortable childhood followed by a more difficult school life. She couldn't wait to leave high school; but didn't know what she had wanted to do. She joined an expat club and worked on the front desk whilst she discovered herself. All she knew for sure was that she wanted to provide for her family.

She has recently re-discovered her strong passion for baking, which she has had since a child. Her latest baking inspiration stems from her European adventures, visiting the various markets, delicatessens and sampling all the tasty treats. She is now married and living in Singapore with her husband and looking to open her high tea workshop where she will also provide one-on-one baking classes.

Made in the USA
Charleston, SC
13 January 2017